THE STUDENT GUIDE TO MINDFULNESS

Sara Miller McCune founded SAGE Publishing in 1965 to support the dissemination of usable knowledge and educate a global community. SAGE publishes more than 1000 journals and over 800 new books each year, spanning a wide range of subject areas. Our growing selection of library products includes archives, data, case studies and video. SAGE remains majority owned by our founder and after her lifetime will become owned by a charitable trust that secures the company's continued independence.

Los Angeles | London | New Delhi | Singapore | Washington DC | Melbourne

THE
STUDENT GUIDE TO
MINDFULNESS

DAVID
MAIR

Los Angeles | London | New Delhi
Singapore | Washington DC | Melbourne

Los Angeles | London | New Delhi
Singapore | Washington DC | Melbourne

SAGE Publications Ltd
1 Oliver's Yard
55 City Road
London EC1Y 1SP

SAGE Publications Inc.
2455 Teller Road
Thousand Oaks, California 91320

SAGE Publications India Pvt Ltd
B 1/I 1 Mohan Cooperative Industrial Area
Mathura Road
New Delhi 110 044

SAGE Publications Asia-Pacific Pte Ltd
3 Church Street
#10-04 Samsung Hub
Singapore 049483

© David Mair 2019

First published 2019

Editor: James Clark
Assistant editor: Diana Alves
Production editor: Martin Fox
Copyeditor: Neil Dowden
Proofreader: Diana Chambers
Indexer: Gary Kirby
Marketing manager: Catherine Slinn
Design: Naomi Robinson
Typeset by: C&M Digitals (P) Ltd, Chennai, India
Printed in the UK

Library of Congress Control Number: 2019932833

British Library Cataloguing in Publication data

A catalogue record for this book is available from the British Library

ISBN 978-1-5264-6322-7
ISBN 978-1-5264-6323-4 (pbk)

In loving memory of my partner,
David Rogers, who taught me to

'**JUST
LET IT
HAPPEN.**,

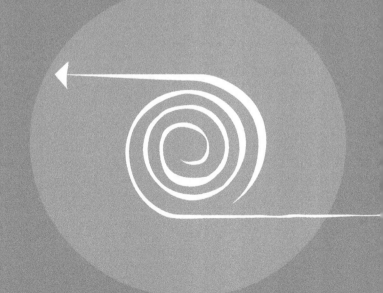

CONTENTS

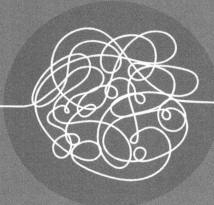

ABOUT THE AUTHOR

DR DAVID MAIR is a BACP Senior Accredited Psychotherapist with over twenty years' experience of supporting students in university settings. He has led mindfulness groups for university staff and students, and believes – from his own experience as well as that of many others – that mindfulness offers a counter-cultural way out of suffering where awareness of self-imposed limitations, anxieties and fears has the potential to lead to greater freedom. Now semi-retired, he maintains a private therapy practice and continues to explore the impact of mindfulness on deep-seated emotions that arise from some of life's most stressful situations.

ABOUT THE ONLINE RESOURCES

THE STUDENT GUIDE TO MINDFULNESS is supported by a range of downloadable resources available at https://study.sagepub.com/mindfulness.

If you are a student:

- MINDFULNESS PODCASTS: Audio versions of key mindfulness exercises from the book, allowing you to take an active part in becoming mindful as you read.

If you work in student support services:

- WEEKLY MINDFULNESS SESSION OUTLINES: These will help you to plan and run 4 x 90-minute mindfulness workshops for students, based around the structure of the book.

- SESSION POWERPOINTS: These editable presentation slides will support you when leading sessions on mindfulness.

'ALL OF HUMANITY'S
PROBLEMS
STEM FROM MAN'S
INABILITY TO
SIT QUIETLY
IN A ROOM ALONE. ,

Blaise Pascal,
Pascal's Pensées (1958)

1
MINDFULNESS
AND
ITS BENEFITS

IN THIS CHAPTER YOU WILL:

- gain an initial understanding of what mindfulness is – and isn't;

- see how mindfulness is a way of being, rather than simply a technique to apply to problems;

- appreciate how mindfulness can enhance your experience of life, not only as a student, but more generally too.

Sophie is a busy student, enjoying her first time of living away from home, meeting new people and getting to grips with a demanding course. She finds the days whizz past so quickly she barely has time to appreciate everything that she is experiencing. Sometimes, when she goes to bed at night, she thinks: 'What have I done today? It barely seems five minutes since I was getting up.' Sophie is allowing herself to experience student life to the full: she loves socialising and she works hard too. However, she sometimes has a sense of being carried along by a fast-moving river, that she is not really in control of what is happening to her. From time to time, she wonders whether some of the people she is meeting are really her types, and whether she should be more able to say 'No' to some of the invitations she gets. Sometimes she also feels exhausted. She wishes that she could step out of the river onto solid ground, just to take stock – to appraise everything that is happening, and to have a stronger sense of feeling grounded, more present in her life – more of a driver of the bus rather than a passenger. A friend has started going to a mindfulness group and wants Sophie to join her, but Sophie has no idea what mindfulness is, why she should go and what might happen if she does. Her friend seems to think it's really helpful, but Sophie is reluctant to take on yet another commitment. She would like answers to her questions.

WHAT IS MINDFULNESS AND HOW CAN IT HELP ME AS A STUDENT?

These are good questions for a busy student to ask. More than likely, like Sophie, you've come across mindfulness in different contexts: it's a new buzzword and there are more and more books on the subject, from mindful colouring books, to mindful bee-keeping, mindful baking and mindful running. But with everything else you have to do as a student, is it really worth making the effort to find out about and practise mindfulness? And if it is, how can you do that?

Mindfulness has emerged in the West over the last thirty years or so, principally from Eastern philosophy and in particular Buddhism. It is just one aspect of the Buddhist eight-fold path to enlightenment (or nirvana). Because it was not, in its original context, intended to be practised as a stand-alone concept, we have to be careful in the West that we don't ignore other equally important aspects of that eight-fold path such as 'right living' or 'right speech'. Mindfulness was never, and should never be, seen as an end in itself, a kind of spiritual navel-gazing: unless it is part of a deeper philosophy of living, it's unlikely that it will be something you find particularly helpful or life-enhancing.

But what is mindfulness? The most common definitions describe it as a way of paying attention, in this moment, to whatever thoughts, feelings or bodily sensations we are experiencing, without judging or trying to stop them. For a while, we step outside our automatic ways of reacting to life and become observers or witnesses of our internal and external world: this helps us develop more helpful ways of responding to ourselves, our problems and neuroses and, just as important, more helpful ways of responding to others, their problems and their neuroses. Key to this more helpful way of responding is the development of self-compassion (and other-compassion).

Mindfulness is similar to, but not the same as, concentration. Imagine that you are walking through a beautiful wood, following an easy path, not thinking about anything in particular, just relaxed and enjoying the day. Then the path takes you to a deep, fast-flowing river. There is no bridge and the only way across the water is over some rather small stepping stones. You can see that the stones are spaced just a little too widely for you, and you also notice that the river is very deep in the middle. As you take your first hesitant step across the river, your mind is intensely focused on what you are doing: you are assessing every movement you make, testing each stone before committing yourself to it, trying to keep your balance. Everything else around you disappears from your mind as you try to make sure you don't fall into the river. This is not mindfulness. This is concentration.

Now imagine that in the middle of the river there is a large, flat stone where you can stop, relax and take stock of how you are doing. As you step onto this rock, you relax a bit and tune in to the sound of the river; you notice the sparkling water rushing past you; you sense the warmth of the sun on your body; you hear some birds singing on the riverbank; you notice your heart beating quite fast and sense your breath moving in and out of your body more quickly than usual. You look around; you *notice* that you are looking around, and you are *aware* of standing on a rock in the middle of a river. And you realise that although crossing this river is quite difficult and that you are a bit worried about actually making it to the other side without getting wet, you accept that this is how things are and wishing for them to be different is not helpful. *This* is mindfulness: awareness of yourself; of thoughts, sounds and sights and bodily sensations; and acceptance of things just as they are right now – even if they are not entirely as you wish they might be.

The four key concepts of mindfulness that we'll be exploring and practising in this book are:

- awareness and acceptance of thoughts, feelings and bodily sensations;
- realisation that we are not *just* our thoughts, feelings and bodily sensations, but that we are also the awareness that contains those thoughts, feelings and sensations;
- development of compassion towards our human vulnerability and frailty (and that of other people);
- familiarisation with the way our minds work, the stories they can create about life, ways they can lead us into unhelpful patterns of living and how we can begin to free ourselves from those stories and patterns.

IF I PRACTISE MINDFULNESS, WILL I BE A MORE SUCCESSFUL STUDENT?

Unfortunately, in its translation into Western culture, mindfulness has too often been presented as another tool for self-improvement, greater success and enhanced productivity. It seems that in the West, the only way we know how to justify an activity is by measuring *improvement*: greater fitness, more calm, more influence, higher profits, more, more and more. Think about your own life for a moment. Since the day you were born, it's likely that you've been measured against innumerable standards to determine whether you are 'normal', whether you are succeeding in life, and how you are doing when measured against your peer group. Height, weight, IQ, exams, interview results – and more. With social media playing such a huge part in many people's lives, our field of comparison has broadened enormously. In previous years, people only had the others who lived on their street or in their village to compare themselves with; now, we have endless airbrushed, Photoshopped images, alongside unrealistic, unattainable images of wealth and success via Facebook, Twitter, Instagram, and so on. No wonder so many of us suffer from what one author calls 'the trance of unworthiness' (Brach, 2013). We berate ourselves continually because we don't look as good as we think we should, we're not as confident as we think we should be and we aren't as successful as we want to be. We have turned into a neurotic, anxiety-driven generation, never satisfied and often looking in the wrong places to feel better about ourselves – such as plastic surgery or expensive consumer goods.

Not surprisingly, then, many people who come to mindfulness hope that it will be a magic bullet to finally help them to feel *permanently* calm, to develop a Zen-like peace that is never disturbed whatever outer circumstances they are facing, or to be able, once and for all, to switch off their anxiety-provoking, depression-inducing thoughts. It's fine to have those hopes. However, being completely honest, mindfulness is *not* a magic bullet that will, if practised hard enough, deliver an eternal inner peace while at the same time enabling you to absorb academic material faster and more easily. Sorry, that's the bad news.

Mindfulness, as I see it and as I have practised it, is best approached with as few expectations as possible, at least in terms of the kind of outcomes you hope it will deliver. Paradoxically, the harder we try to 'get it right', the less we are likely to feel it is worthwhile or to experience any benefits. In that sense, we might be better to approach mindfulness rather as we approach going to sleep: when we go to bed at night, most of us don't lie there thinking, 'I hope this sleep makes me a better person', or 'If I just sleep in the right position, maybe I'll be a calmer person'. You've probably had the experience of lying awake at night, desperately trying to make yourself fall asleep, but realising that the harder you try, the more awake you feel. Trying too hard with mindfulness suggests an anxiety to 'get it right', or to achieve a certain state of being – which is likely to backfire. But unlike going to bed in order to sleep, mindfulness can be thought of as 'falling awake' – coming back to our senses and reconnecting with the present moment, stepping out of our thinking, emotional, instinctive minds.

Another way of thinking about mindfulness would be to think of it like going for a walk just for the pleasure of it, rather than trying to get somewhere specific. There's a big difference in walking for pleasure and walking with the specific aim of getting fitter, reaching a particular destination or covering a fixed distance in a certain amount time. For me, the first kind of walk is the most enjoyable. Every day I set off for a pleasurable walk with my dog, Harry. I have a general sense of the route we're going to cover and how long I expect to be out for, but I allow myself just to enjoy whatever arises as we walk: sounds, sights, smells, meeting other people (and dogs), and occasional unexpected treasures such as seeing a kingfisher flash past on the river. Harry and I become absorbed in the moment – he in his doggy way and I in my human way. We are not trying to get anywhere in particular or feel a particular way; we walk in the rain and the sun, and some walks are more enjoyable than others. Harry runs around, sniffing, exploring, fully 'in the moment', not worrying about what time we're going to get home or whether I'll feed him tonight. Sometimes, I see people running past us, gasping, red in the face, clutching water bottles, timing themselves, seeing how many steps they can cram into thirty minutes. How different is their experience of the same route. There are also some times when I come back from our walk and realise that I've experienced very little of what was going on in the world around us, because I was completely lost in my thoughts: worrying, regretting, fretting, planning, dreaming, scheming.

So mindfulness is *not*, primarily, about achieving any particular state of mind, or stopping thoughts, or clearing your mind. It's *not* about emptying your mind so that you can sit like a statue, empty of feelings and desires. Instead, it is about deliberately and consciously stepping off the hamster wheel of incessant achievement, and it's about stopping trying to always get somewhere, or make things better. It's about tuning in to what is going on right here, right now, both within ourselves and around us. We deliberately 'wake up' from autopilot and tune in for a period of time to the world around and within us: we stop 'doing' and allow ourselves to just 'be'.

MINDFUL EXERCISE

Just for a few moments, see what happens when you deliberately and consciously direct your attention away from the outside world and turn inwards to sensations in your body. Tune in to the feeling of your breath: you are breathing all the time, but are rarely aware of this. It is an automatic process that normally passes you by. For five minutes, see if you can keep your attention focused on your breath. Just five minutes. Gently allow your focus to come away from any worries you may have, any anxiety or concerns – for a few moments, come into your body and out of your thinking mind. Feel your chest and stomach rising and falling, expanding and contracting; notice any gaps between an in-breath and an out-breath. Just notice; don't try to control or change. Each breath is unique, a never-to-be-repeated moment of your life with a different texture, speed and intensity. Your task is simply to become aware of this ever-changing life-giving aspect of your life.

How easy was this for you? It sounds very simple to focus your attention on your breath. However, I'm guessing that, as with most people, you found that your attention started to wander away from your breath fairly quickly and that you began to get caught up in thinking about what you were doing: 'How long have I got to go?' 'What's the point of this?' 'I know he said five minutes, but I think a minute is enough.' 'Am I doing this right?' And so on.

For the moment, simply register your experience of trying this simple exercise. Whether you found it enjoyable, boring, easy or difficult, just notice what your own experience was.

LISTEN TO THE AUDIO CLIP AT
https://study.sagepub.com/mindfulness

WHAT'S THE POINT OF MINDFULNESS IF IT'S NOT ABOUT BEING A CALMER, MORE SUCCESSFUL PERSON?

This is another good question. Again, we have to realise that this question also arises from our achievement-obsessed culture. We find it baffling that we might engage in something simply *because* it is not achievement-orientated, that setting aside some regular time to just *be*, rather than always *doing*, might, in and of itself, be profitable. Repeatedly, I've seen students give up on mindfulness because they feel it's not getting them anywhere fast, that it's not dealing with their anxiety or depression, or turning them into super-efficient workers who will get top marks for every assignment.

One helpful metaphor from mindfulness teacher Suryacitta, which I find extremely helpful, is to think of mindfulness as 'a container for our emotions and thoughts' (Suryacitta, 2014).

Imagine a glass full of water, full to the brim. The glass, the container, represents the current extent of your awareness. The water inside the container represents your emotions, your thoughts, your bodily sensations, your behaviours. Because the glass and the water are so closely matched, it doesn't take much – a slight hurt, an irritation – to jolt the glass and for the water (your feelings) to spill over. Every day we are jolted by things going on in the world around us (you only have to switch on the news to receive several major jolts), and by things going on inside ourselves (memories of past hurts, current conflicts and worries). By the end of each day, we probably end up upset, anxious, depressed – or, to go back to the glass of water metaphor, wet.

When we first approach mindfulness, what we hope for is that the water – our emotions will change and that we will stop getting so upset by the things that happen around us, that we will stop feeling anxious or depressed. So many people say, when asked why they are interested in mindfulness, 'I want to be calm in all situations', or 'I want to stop feeling anxious all the time', or 'I want to stop being so upset by what other people say to me'. They hope for an almost zombie-like existence where they are never troubled by basic human feelings. That would be a tragedy, because if that were possible, they would, in fact, be less than human. Mindfulness should not be seen as an escape route from life, or a way of somehow switching off normal, basic human emotions – even those we find uncomfortable such as fear or anger; it is, in fact, the opposite. Mindfulness helps us to turn towards whatever is happening in our lives, to sit with it, even if sometimes that is quite painful or difficult. We learn to accept or befriend our emotions, thoughts and bodily sensations, and to stop judging them, which only makes things worse. We embrace our lives as they are with self-compassion and acceptance.

Now, while mindfulness is not a quick fix for powerful or troubling emotions, it will, over time – and we're talking months, not weeks – begin to change how we *relate* to our powerful feelings. In this sense, going back to our metaphor of the glass of water, what we are changing is the glass, not the water. Mindfulness enables us to create a bigger container for our difficult emotions so that, even though we may still get upset, anxious or depressed, we are somehow able to accept and allow those emotions to exist with greater equanimity and compassion for ourselves and other people.

After a long time of practising mindfulness, it is likely that our emotions will change too; we may find that we don't react so strongly to difficult situations and that we have more compassion for ourselves and others. However, initially, this should not be our primary aim for practising. Instead, we should try, as far as possible, to regard mindfulness as a wonderful opportunity to step out of our automatic-thinking minds and reconnect with the immediacy of the world around us, to wake up from the 'trance of unworthiness', and simply savour some moments of awareness and connection with life. It is, ultimately, about taking better care of ourselves, other people and the world around us.

CAN ANYONE PRACTISE MINDFULNESS? I'VE TRIED BEFORE AND I GAVE UP BECAUSE I COULDN'T CLEAR MY MIND

Basically, yes, anyone can practise mindfulness because it is a fundamental human ability – indeed, perhaps one of the hallmarks of what it means to be human. As far as we know, no other animal species is able to be *aware* of the fact that it is thinking, or experiencing an emotion: *to be aware of being aware*. Chimpanzees clearly have sophisticated thinking processes and they undoubtedly experience emotions, but do they have *awareness* of the fact that they are thinking and feeling? Can a chimp reflect on its thoughts and feelings?

Chimp   Hungry! Food! Eat!

Human   I'm quite hungry. I think I'll go and make a snack. [But also:] I'm aware that I'm feeling quite hungry and that I'd like a snack. But I'm also trying to lose weight, so I'll resist for a while and wait until supper time.

Humans are able to be *aware that we are conscious*, and to be aware of, to observe, the content of our thinking minds. This is, as far as we know, a unique ability and central to the practice of mindfulness. If you have tried mindfulness previously but given up because you felt that you were not 'cut out for it', that your mind simply wanders too much, then you may have misunderstood the purpose and the process of mindfulness. I hope that by the time you have worked through several of the exercises in this book, you will be clearer about the truth that a wandering mind is not a sign that you cannot practise mindfulness; your awareness of the fact that your mind is wandering merely confirms that you are practising mindfulness already.

IS THERE ANYONE WHO REALLY CAN'T BENEFIT FROM MINDFULNESS?

This is an important question: whether everyone can practise and *benefit* from mindfulness. Are there any kinds of issues that mean that people would best avoid it? Again, in the rush to promote mindfulness in our culture, there are too few considerations given to the fact that it is not a panacea for all ills and may actually be unhelpful for some people. Because formal mindfulness practices require us to sit still and tune in to whatever is going on inside us, and to witness thoughts, feelings and bodily sensations, there are indeed some people who may be advised not to try this – at least not without ongoing professional support. If any of the following issues apply to you, you would be better not to engage in formal mindfulness practices without professional support from a therapist or a mindfulness teacher who is also skilled in responding to mental health concerns.

- You are suffering from the aftermath of trauma from a recent or past event, including physical, emotional or sexual abuse.
- You are dealing with intense grief or loss.
- You are experiencing psychosis.
- You are in the midst of a deep depression.

Even in these situations, you may still find engaging with *informal* mindfulness practices helpful (see Chapter 3 for more about formal and informal mindfulness) but, again, you would be best advised to seek professional therapeutic support for underlying concerns.

This underscores a very important point: mindfulness is not a substitute for psychological support and therapy. There are some experiences and emotions that are simply too powerful for us to deal with alone. Sometimes we need medical or psychological support to deal with the impact of certain life events, especially those involving intense physical responses. Please don't look to mindfulness alone to deal with those experiences; you may well need ongoing therapeutic support to help you safely process what has happened.

I DON'T UNDERSTAND HOW MINDFULNESS IS GOING TO HELP ME AS A STUDENT

Ultimately, only you will be able to decide if mindfulness is going to be something you wish to incorporate into your life. It's important to realise that reading about mindfulness can never be a substitute for simply trying it for yourself. In that sense, it's like reading about doing exercise, as opposed to actually doing exercise. Reading can give you pointers but it can never, by itself, enable you to know what it is actually like.

Here is an example of how mindfulness might be of benefit for a student:

Andy is a final-year student. All through his studies he's struggled with anxiety, never really believing that he is good enough or that he's done enough work. His anxiety has led him to avoid doing work, or attend lectures, and this means that he's fallen behind in his work which has, in turn, made his anxiety worse. Andy has always wanted to get rid of his anxiety, to feel more confident and more in control of his life. After some counselling, which has helped him to understand how anxiety works and how it can become a self-fulfilling prophecy ('I know I'll feel anxious, so I won't go to lectures; but then I'll miss lectures and feel more anxious'), Andy has been attending a short mindfulness group to learn some basic practices that he's been incorporating into his life. He spends a few minutes each morning sitting in bed, tuning into his breath, and to whatever is going on in his body. He has learnt to notice his anxious thoughts when they arise, and he is getting better at observing them rather than getting caught up in them. He's learnt that his thoughts are quite repetitive and that they are not 'the truth', and that he can allow himself to feel anxiety in his body without adding to it by unhelpful self-talk ('I can't stand this! I am such an idiot for feeling like this – what's wrong with me?' or 'Unless I feel free from anxiety, there's no point in me doing any work'). Andy is beginning to understand that the way the human brain works is not fully within his control and that his anxiety response is not unique to him. Rather than beating himself up for getting anxious, he is starting to be more self-compassionate and can say to himself: 'It's OK, Andy – you're anxious and that's OK. You can handle this. Don't beat yourself up, just take some deep breaths – this is difficult for you, but you can cope. You're not alone in feeling like this.' Andy has started to practise mindful walking and he really likes this because it enables him to focus on the outside world and, when his anxious thoughts carry him away, to gently come back to his physical senses. Rather than always sticking his earphones on when he's walking around campus, he slows down and tunes in to whatever he can see, hear and feel. Of course, he still gets anxious in some situations, but rather than seeing this as something to get rid of, to blank out, or as something 'wrong' with him, he is beginning to see his reactions as understandable and something he can handle better. Mindfulness is helping Andy to take better care of himself and to make choices that are more likely to guide him towards achieving the best he can with his current internal and external resources.

This book will not ask you to devote hours of your time to mindfulness practice. Sometimes, we can be made to feel that unless we commit one hundred per cent to something we are not taking it seriously enough. My hope, by contrast, is that you will find enough here to intrigue you and encourage you to have a go at some aspects of mindfulness, and that some of the psychological insights will enrich whatever you decide to try. Nevertheless, it's worth saying that, as with anything, you will only really discover how mindfulness can support you by giving it a real chance. Only you can decide what that looks like for you, and I would say that in terms of formal practice, five or ten consistent minutes a day are better than forty inconsistent ones. You may find the informal practices easier to incorporate into your daily life, but they will generally make more sense and be more helpful if they are based on at least some formal practice each week.

To summarise:

Mindfulness *is not*:

- a magic bullet that will enable you to always feel calm, peaceful and untroubled;
- a no-effort technique to banish anxiety or depression;
- a guaranteed way to achieve amazing academic results all the time.

However, mindfulness *is*:

- an opportunity to step out of autopilot and reconnect with life as it is in this moment;
- a way to develop greater familiarity with your own – and others' – thoughts, emotions and bodily sensations so that you can respond more compassionately;
- a way to enable you to be more present in your life and to 'wake up' from the trance of worry, anxiety or depression;
- a chance to avoid creating additional suffering for yourself when you encounter painful events in life;
- a pathway that can bring ever increasing benefits to you as you learn to relate to your life with the wisdom that non-reactivity generates.

QUESTIONS FOR REFLECTION

1. What intrigues you about mindfulness and what are your hopes and expectations as you approach it? What criteria will you use to assess how beneficial the practices are for you?

2. If mindfulness is a way of living rather than a technique for achieving success, how does this affect your thoughts about making time to learn about it and to practise it in your daily life?

3. At this point, how might you explain what mindfulness is to a friend who asks you about it? Can you use your own words to describe what it is and isn't?

FURTHER READING

Thich Nhat Hahn (2008) *The Miracle of Mindfulness: The Classic Guide to Meditation by the World's Most Revered Master.* London: Rider.

A gentle, compassionate and enticing introduction to the simplicity and depths of mindfulness by a Zen Buddhist.

Ruby Wax (2014) *Sane New World.* London: Hodder.

A practical and humorous introduction to mindfulness written by someone who speaks personally of the benefits of mindfulness in daily life.

REFERENCES

Brach, T. (2013) *True Refuge: Finding Peace and Freedom in Your Own Awakened Heart.* Carlsbad, CA: Hay House.

Pascal, B. ([1670] 1958) *Pascal's Pensées.* New York: E.P. Dutton.

Suryacitta (2014) The ABC of Mindfulness. Available at: www.youtube.com/watch?v=x97dTzxB1zY (accessed 13 January 2019).

"WE HUMANS ARE CREATURES OF HABIT; OUR BRAINS ARE WIRED TO THINK THE SAME THOUGHTS AGAIN AND AGAIN LIKE A BROKEN RECORD. MOST OF THESE HABITUAL THOUGHTS ARE DUALISTIC AND NEGATIVE. WE ARE OBSESSED WITH LABELING THINGS GOOD OR BAD, RIGHT OR WRONG. ONLY VERY RARELY DO WE CHANGE OUR MINDS ABOUT THESE PRE-DETERMINED, FIXED ASSUMPTIONS. OBVIOUSLY, THIS LIMITS OUR ABILITY TO BE CREATIVE AND THINK OUTSIDE THE BOX!"

Richard Rohr (2018)

2
MINDFULNESS
AND
THE BRAIN

IN THIS
CHAPTER
YOU WILL:

- gain awareness of how the human brain has evolved and how many of its functions are beyond our conscious control;

- understand the concept of 'monkey mind' as a metaphor for the associative way our thinking minds work;

- appreciate the need for compassion as we approach mindfulness with our powerful, primitive brain.

Dana is a newly arrived first-year student and she is struggling to settle into her new campus accommodation. Home is a small village where she went to school and had a good group of local friends. Mum and dad, a younger brother, and a pet cat and dog are all at home and Dana misses them a lot. She is feeling highly anxious and can't understand why. Sleep is hard; there is an almost constant feeling of threat, nothing feels natural or normal. Everything takes effort and is tiring. Dana thinks a lot about home and family: the contrast with a small, fairly noisy bedroom in a hall of residence is enormous and Dana is not sure she will be able to adapt to the new environment. The feeling of homesickness and anxiety leaves Dana wondering whether she can stay at university or should think of leaving. Dana has never felt like this before. Everyone else seems to be coping better than they are; it's all upsetting and puzzling, and it's starting to feel too much.

THE HUMAN BRAIN: PRIMITIVE YET SOPHISTICATED DRIVER OF THOUGHTS, FEELINGS AND BEHAVIOURS

Before you start to use some of the mindfulness practices described in this book, it's important to have some understanding of why, although the practices are very simple, it can be harder than you imagine to persevere with them, or to feel that you are able to sustain the practice of mindfulness over a long period of time. One simple fact to hold on to if you struggle to practise mindfulness, or to see any value in it, is just this:

Mindfulness is simple – but not easy.

You and I are human beings and so we share very similar thoughts and feelings; if that weren't so, we wouldn't be able to understand each other or communicate. We go through similar stages of growth – physical and emotional – and we tend to behave in predictable ways in certain situations. Ultimately, we are who we are because we have a human brain.

The human brain is a thing of wonder. Described by some as the most complex organism in the universe, neuroscientists and psychologists are still unravelling its physical properties and functioning. Without a doubt, it is an amazing thing to be able to write an essay, drinking a cup of scalding hot coffee without burning your lips while listening to music, while simultaneously daydreaming about a forthcoming date. The human brain has enabled us to fly at supersonic speeds, send men to the moon, discover cures for illnesses that would once have killed millions and play Pokémon Go. Equally, the human brain has created unimaginable suffering as we have fought against each other in terrible wars, denied basic rights to millions because of racism and sexism, and has the potential to ensnare us in addiction and depression.

Human consciousness, which arises from the physical workings of the brain, is another miracle that scientists and philosophers still ponder and debate. What, exactly, is consciousness? What is it that enables us to be aware? And to be aware that we are aware? This ability – unique among species on earth – is part of what makes us the amazing, terrible species that we are. We do not react to life simply from instinct, but are able to consider our actions, and to contemplate our thoughts and emotions. As far as we know, chimps don't have this capacity, even though they can appear so similar to us in their behaviours at times.

How is all of this relevant to our practice of mindfulness? Actually, it's fundamental. Human consciousness is the basis from which mindfulness can emerge. If our brains are damaged in some way and we lose our ability to focus, or undergo a personality change, then our ability to practise mindfulness may be seriously compromised. If we are under the influence of alcohol, drugs or other addictive substances, we will not be able to practise mindfulness as described in this book. Consciousness is a precious gift that we take for granted most of the time, but it is the road we travel along as we incorporate mindfulness into our lives.

THE TRIUNE BRAIN

I need to be clear that I'm not a neuroscientist. My understanding of how the brain works is basic, but one way of appreciating how our brains work that I've found helpful is the triune brain model (MacLean, 1990). This describes our brains as made up of three parts which have evolved at different times over millions of years: a 'lower' reptilian, instinctive brain; a 'middle', limbic, emotional brain, and a 'higher', analytical, conscious brain, the neo-cortex. These are not separate brains, but have evolved separately and now operate interdependently, often in ways we don't realise, and frequently in ways beyond our control.

The *reptilian* part of our brains is the part that emerged earliest, in evolutionary terms. Some have called it 'lizard brain' because its functions are the same as those manifested by simple creatures that have existed for millions of years at a basic level. It's a powerful part of our brains, taking care of many essential functions that keep us alive: our breathing, sending electrical impulses to keep our hearts beating, regulating body temperature. It is, fundamentally, concerned with our survival. It drives the 'fight, flight or freeze' response we all experience in threatening situations, and is supersensitive to changes in our environment that may signal threat. Someone has described this part of our brain as concerned only with four 'F's': fleeing, fighting, feeding and ... reproducing (Armstrong, 2011). These are deeply ingrained and hardwired survival instincts, shared by all human beings in every part of the world. We can't turn these instincts off (thank goodness, or we'd never keep breathing when we're asleep), but we can, through mindfulness, become more familiar with our instinctive reactions and develop awareness of how they can often lead to unhelpful or inappropriate responses in modern-world situations. Our brains evolved to cope with a very different world from the one we all inhabit now. They are not good at distinguishing between real threats and imagined ones, and they make all kinds of errors in processing our experience of the outside world, which is very useful to know, as we shall see.

The middle part of the brain, the *'limbic'* brain, emerged in the first mammals. You may have heard of structures within the brain such as the hippocampus and the amygdala: these are two key parts of this area of the brain. They are responsible for our memories and our emo-tions: all of us are subject to various unconscious biases in our evaluation and judgement of other people, and this part of our brains is responsible for those judgements and evaluations. As with the reptilian part of the brain, much of what happens in the limbic brain occurs outside our awareness; it happens automatically and we can be said to be on autopilot when we are operating mainly from this region of our brains. Regular, repetitive actions get stored here so that we can perform them with as little effort as necessary – getting dressed, walking, driving, giving presentations. New routines can feel very difficult to master at first until they are practised for a long time and then stored in this region of the brain: learning a new piece of music, a new language, juggling, giving confident presentations. The limbic and reptilian parts of the brain interact in new situations quickly and easily, in ways we don't fully control. A new environment with its strange sights, sounds and smells can trigger judgements from the limbic brain ('Don't like this place', 'Don't like him/her') which in turn trigger reptilian brain responses – fight/flight/freeze – that may not be helpful to us as we seek to mature and develop new skills and abilities. When you move into new accommodation, especially if you are living with strangers, you will, almost inevitably, be on high alert, with your emotional threat system switched 'on', simply because your brain is making sense of all the new inputs it is receiving. Often, we can wish that our emotions were other than what they are: we hate feeling anxious, or sad, or angry. Yet, being emotional is a key part of our human experience. If we cannot access our emotions, or express them honestly, our sense of being part of life can be greatly diminished.

The 'higher' brain, the *neocortex*, is the most recent to emerge in evolutionary terms. This part of our brains is what enables us to learn, imagine and engage in abstract thought and reasoning. Human culture has arisen because of this part of the brain, in all its amazing diversity around the world. The neocortex is responsible for language and for dimensions of human experience such as spirituality, literature, dance and music. It possesses an almost limitless capacity to learn and to be flexible. This part of the brain is what makes us truly human. Yet, as with the reptilian and limbic brains, the neocortex does not operate in isolation. It can be powerfully influenced by the reptilian brain: if the reptilian brain, with its basic survival drive, is too dominant, then the neocortex can become obsessed with matters such as security, or be driven by anxiety-provoking thoughts that stop us from taking appropriate risks in life. Or it can create weapons of mass destruction which it believes will calm the territorial anxieties emanating from the reptilian brain. Zombie knives (where complex imaginative and manufacturing processes are put to work in the service of aggressive, territory-defending instincts) are a tragic outcome of the reptilian and neocortex parts of the brain operating in tandem, with the reptilian brain dominating. The work of doctors and surgeons working in war zones (where natural fear of harm is set aside in order to serve higher human values of care and healing) is an example of the two areas of the brain working together, with the neocortex dominating.

MINDFUL EXERCISE

How familiar are you with your triune brain and with how it impacts on your experience of reality? If we are not aware, life can become dominated and controlled by emotions and thoughts generated automatically by our reptilian brain.

Take a moment now to reflect on any situations you are facing that are likely to trigger your reptilian brain and its flight, flight, freeze reactions. New accommodation? New campus? New town? New housemates? Anything new is likely to activate those primitive survival responses. How about any threats that you feel at the moment? Exams? Presentations? Relationships?

Primitive brain will likely generate intense physical sensations when activated: the adrenalin released into your system can lead to dizziness, sickness, rapid heartbeat.

Sit quietly for a moment; close your eyes if you are comfortable. Take some slow, deep breaths. Allow yourself to bring a threatening situation you are facing to come to mind – perhaps not the most difficult, but one that generates some emotional or physical reaction. Our typical reaction is to avoid these feelings; but you can, instead, sit with them and name the emotions or sensations as they arise: 'This is fear', 'This is dread', 'This is a churning stomach'. And then, when you have identified these feelings, continuing with a reassurance to yourself: 'This is fear – and that's a normal reaction (when moving into new accommodation)', 'This is dread – and this is completely understandable (when making an important presentation)', 'This is a churning stomach – and everyone feels this (when they're going for an interview)'.

The simple act of acknowledging how *normal* your feelings and thoughts are allows you to apply mindful awareness to what might otherwise remain hidden and, because of being hidden, more powerfully distressing: 'This is normal: my brain is simply doing its job to protect me. These feelings are not pleasant but they will not harm me. Other people feel the same. In time, these feelings will pass. I am safe; I am OK.' By reassuring yourself that your feelings are normal, you can avoid feeding the primitive brain with unhelpful thoughts and stories: 'I feel anxious – and this is normal', 'I feel sad – and that's a normal reaction in these circumstances'.

Over the next few days and weeks, at any point where you recognise that powerful feelings have been triggered in you – especially any that are distressing – tune in to that feeling and simply acknowledge to yourself that your wonderful, powerful, instinctive brain is at work trying to protect you as best it can.

LISTEN TO THE AUDIO CLIP AT
https://study.sagepub.com/mindfulness

Although the triune model of the human brain does not provide a detailed neurological insight into brain functioning, it's one that I've found helpful in understanding my own thoughts, feelings and behaviours. And it's a model I'll be making reference to as we begin to practise mindfulness.

It's so important to be aware that our brains are powerful, often instinctive, organisms over which we don't have full, conscious control. We are all subject to the survival instincts and drives of the reptilian brain; we all make snap judgements about people and situations because of memories and pathways built up in the limbic brain; and we all are capable of amazing kindness and hideous cruelty because of our imaginative capacities derived from the neocortex. None of this changes as we practise mindfulness. But what can, and does, change is our *awareness* of what we are feeling, thinking and doing. We are able to tap into our human consciousness: to simply observe what is going on inside and around us – not judging it, or trying to stop it, or change it (at least, not while we are practising mindfulness). We slowly develop a greater awareness of patterns of thinking, feeling and behaving, and, over time, the capacity to be less dominated by those patterns that are unhelpful to us as we seek to mature and live good lives. We develop a greater capacity to *respond* to life (in accordance with our values) rather than simply *reacting* to it (from a fear-based reptilian brain). We become freer to make choices that reduce our own and others' suffering.

MINDFULNESS, AWARENESS AND SELF-COMPASSION

One personal example of how mindfulness has helped me is that by sitting quietly, consciously bringing my attention to my breath, I became aware of how often my mind drifted away into imagined arguments. I discovered that I very quickly get drawn into a kind of soap opera fight with someone I imagine has slighted me or upset me; I have discovered that there is an aggressive, often angry part of me that is quick to take offence or to move swiftly to 'fight' mode. Mindfulness has helped me to accept this part of myself and to be able to recognise it for what it is: the reptilian brain at work, defending territory, seeking survival, ready to attack anything it imagines is threatening its safety.

There is something to hold in mind, too. If you are a man aged under twenty-five, your brain is not yet fully physically developed. If you are a woman aged under twenty-one, your brain is not yet fully physically developed (Nagel, 2017). This is something that we generally do not realise, and yet it is vital if we are to develop self-and-other compassion. It's impossible to overstate the importance of our brains in determining who we are, how we feel and how we live. But most typical undergraduate students at colleges and universities have brains that are still being formed. This has important consequences:

- You may sleep more than older adults (brain formation is very tiring).
- Your moods may swing more than older adults (your hard-wiring is still being constructed – 'work in progress').
- Your sense of identity may fluctuate (you are still discovering who you are, and who you want to be – don't expect to think the same way you did when you were twenty-one when you are forty-five).

Being a student typically happens at one of the most demanding times of your developmental life. Your brain is undergoing transformation. Your body is changing. Sexuality is becoming a much greater concern (remember the reptilian brain and the four Fs? No one is immune). You are starting to interact with much larger groups of people at college, at work, in the world around you (and your reptilian brain may well feel highly threatened by these groups and by the new environments you find yourself in).

So we come back, again, to self-compassion. These years are not always easy years, and you are not to blame. None of us had a choice about being born as a human being, or about being subject to the limitations of our human brain. Of course, we live in an amazing world, and our capacities are truly awesome as a species. But much can, and does, go wrong, and one of the most powerful ways in which things go wrong is when we start to criticise ourselves, put ourselves down (or do that to others) simply because we are all dealing with the biggest challenge of all: being human.

Mindfulness offers us a different perspective from which to view our human lives, with all their opportunities and limitations. We all have tendencies to avoid situations we perceive as threatening and to live only for our own benefit – to succumb to the lower brain with its fear-based survival instincts. But we all have great capacities to make contributions to this world while we are alive – to rise above the fear-based instincts and develop compassion for ourselves and those we live with.

MONKEY MIND

It should be clear, then, that our brains are extremely complex and amazing organisms that we are not in full conscious control of. Yet until this is pointed out to us, we may believe that our perceptions, our opinions and our thoughts are the truth. Friendships have ended, careers have been lost and marriages ended in bitter divorce simply because we tend to believe too easily that we have a grip on the truth that others do not. I recommend that anyone who overestimates their own grasp on reality (all of us?) should read books about the many ways we routinely overestimate our own memories, our own abilities and perceptions, and our own opinions. *Being Wrong: Adventures in the Margins of Error* by Kathryn Schulz is an excellent, if sobering, analysis of how frequently and easily we deceive ourselves yet remain convinced we are right.

Our minds are not fully under our control either. As anyone who has struggled with anxiety or depression knows, none of us can simply will upsetting thoughts to stop or change into positive ones. It may be possible, with effort, to challenge and change slightly upsetting thoughts, but when very strong emotions are involved, it becomes less likely that we will achieve this completely.

In Buddhism, there is a term for our wandering, instinctive thoughts: *monkey mind* – a wonderful phrase. To me, it perfectly sums up my own thinking mind. In fact, I would say monkey *minds*; yes – more than one. If I allow myself to simply sit and observe my thoughts (as you will too if you start to practise mindfulness), it isn't long before random memories, worries, fears, anxieties, daydreams, desires and angers start to appear. And these thoughts and images are all associative; one thought triggers another, and another, ad infinitum. One moment I can be sat serenely on my chair being mindful of my breath or of sounds – the next, wham. I am right back in the memory of an argument with a colleague, my heart beating, thinking of what I should have said, and rehearsing what I'll say next time they dare speak to me like that.

Our thoughts are like a troop of monkeys, swinging through the trees. We can't stop them. They are there. Sometimes they're fairly quiet, just the odd hoot. At other times, they are rampaging through the treetops, swinging and chattering loudly, overwhelming us with a bombardment of apparently important, but ultimately random, thoughts and memories.

Everyone has a monkey mind. The truth is that until we wake up and learn to sit and observe our monkey mind, we will be subject to it – pulled this way and that, believing everything it tells us, unable to recognise that the screeches and hoots are not necessarily in our best interests, or helpful to us in being who we aspire to be.

When I was about twelve, I went to a zoo. I was fascinated by the monkeys, chattering in their cages. They looked so human that I could almost believe they were trying to talk to me.

One monkey was very small, so small that it could have sat in the palm of my hand. It looked so sweet, so cute; despite the warning signs, I reached out my hand, hoping to stroke it. As soon as my finger got within striking distance, the monkey reached out and grabbed my finger with a vice-like grip; I could not pull back because its hold was so powerful. A tiny little monkey, but with the power to clamp my finger in its grip until it decided to let go.

So, don't think about taming your monkey mind. Monkeys are too powerful. All we can do is train ourselves to watch our monkey mind at work, sometimes sitting quietly in the corner, at other times screeching and swinging through the trees.

Dana went along to an introductory mindfulness group on campus. Just sitting in a group with other students, many of whom talked about having similar feelings to those that Dana was experiencing, was reassuring in itself. Dana learned that although other students might look confident and self-assured, in fact many were just as anxious as she was. The breathing exercises that the facilitator taught were soothing and calming, and learning about why she was feeling the way she was helped Dana to accept those feelings rather than trying to get rid of them. Dana learned that the change of environment had given her reptilian brain a challenge and that it was simply trying to adjust to the newness of everything around her. The feelings didn't magically disappear, but with awareness, self-compassion and a growing ability to sit with the difficult emotions, Dana was learning to take better care of herself and to be patient as she went through a challenging process of acclimatisation.

QUESTIONS FOR REFLECTION

1. Fight, flight, freeze: do you recognise any of these reactions within yourself when you are facing new to challenging situations? Is one of these more predominant for you than others?

2. With awareness that primitive brain functioning is so powerful, so intuitive and so universal, how might you change your reaction to your own instinctive responses to these situations?

3. Mindfulness offers the opportunity for a deeper awareness of our inner emotions and thoughts about life situations and thereby greater choice about how we react to these. How might this be helpful for you?

FURTHER READING

Ralph de la Rosa (2018) *The Monkey is the Messenger: Meditation and What Your Busy Mind Is Trying to Tell You.* Boulder, CO: Shambhala Publications.

An encouraging guide to responding compassionately and attentively to monkey mind; rather than something to fight against, the author contends that by befriending our thoughts and learning from them, great healing is possible.

David Eagleman (2015) *The Brain: The Story of You.* Edinburgh: Canongate Books.

A fascinating guide to the human brain by a leading neuroscientist. In reading this, you will develop your appreciation for the amazing capacities we so often take for granted.

REFERENCES

Armstrong, K. (2011) *Twelve Steps to a Compassionate Life.* London: Bodley Head.

MacLean, P. (1990) *The Triune Brain in Evolution Role in Paleocerebral Functions.* New York: Springer.

Nagel, M. (2017) What could they be thinking? Understanding the adolescent brain. *University and College Counselling,* March: 4–8.

Rohr, R. (2018) The creative mind of Christ. Available at: https://cac.org/the-creative-mind-of-christ-2018-06-03/ (accessed 16 January 2019).

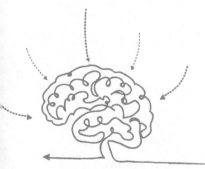

'To **MEDITATE**
IS TO LOOK DEEPLY
AND SEE THE THINGS THAT OTHERS CANNOT SEE,
INCLUDING THE WRONG VIEWS THAT LIE AT
THE BASE OF
OUR SUFFERING.,

Thich Nhat Hanh,
The Art of Living (2017)

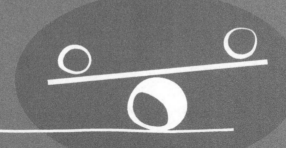

3
MINDFULNESS: FORMAL AND INFORMAL

IN THIS CHAPTER YOU WILL:

- learn about different kinds of mindfulness practice, in particular formal and informal practice;

- see how you can bring mindfulness into virtually every area of your life;

- think about how to build a formal practice that works for you;

- recognise the importance of commitment and intention as you start to build a mindfulness practice.

Greg is a second-year physics student. His course is really tough and demanding. Every night he has worksheets to complete, and every week there is a course test. Worksheets, reading, experiments, revising – the list goes on. Although he really enjoys the subject, he has been feeling overwhelmed with the amount he has to do: his friends all seem to be having a much easier ride than he is, with plenty of free time for sports and socialising. Something of a perfectionist, Greg spends nearly every evening poring over his books, barely taking a break, and falls into bed feeling exhausted – before getting up to repeat it all again the next day. There seems to be no room, no space in his life: it's all work and no fun. Although Greg has heard about mindfulness, and it's something he'd like to explore, he feels that he just doesn't have time for anything else in his life. His only priority is work and staying on top of the demanding workload he has been set.

I wonder what you imagine mindfulness practice consists of? What comes to mind when you think about that? What do you see? Perhaps you think of long sessions, sitting uncomfortably cross-legged, desperately trying to empty your mind so that you achieve a state of enlightenment or nirvana. Maybe you've already tried some mindfulness meditation, possibly with mixed feelings. On the one hand, it might have been quite peaceful and nice; but on the other hand, it might have felt rather boring and time-consuming. In the past, I've asked students to tell me what they think a good mindfulness practice would look like, and it tends to be along these lines:

6am – get up, meditate for an hour

12pm – more meditation (maybe skipping lunch to fit it in)

5.30pm – go to the Buddhist society for a couple of hours; more meditation

9.30pm – another half-hour of meditation before bed

There's a well-known story about a novice Zen monk who approaches the master of his monastery. This monk is super-keen to achieve enlightenment and to rise above the ordinary concerns of everyday life. 'Master, how long must I meditate to achieve enlightenment?', the monk enquires. 'Young one, you must meditate for five hours every day for ten years', comes the reply. 'Well, master', the monk goes on, 'what if I meditate for ten hours every day?' The master pauses and looks into the monk's eyes: 'If you meditate for ten hours, it will take you twenty years.' he says. The wise master knows that it is not *how long* we practise, but the intention and sincerity behind our practice that counts. *Trying too hard* is, paradoxically, a sure-fire way to become discouraged and burnt out. When it comes to all kinds of activities, as humans we have a tendency to either push ourselves too hard, or not push ourselves at all. In practising mindfulness, we must look for *the middle way* – not pushing ourselves too hard, but neither fooling ourselves that spending a few moments with a 'mindful' colouring book is something that is likely to be of much use to us in the long term.

I have been to mindfulness courses where the 'homework' for the first week was to do a fifty-minute body-scan every day. Fifty minutes. Not surprisingly, most people who came back for the second week had either failed to achieve this goal, or pretended that they had achieved it when in fact they'd fallen asleep; and not surprisingly, quite a few people didn't come back at all. Fifty minutes, for someone new to mindfulness, is simply too long and will only lead to feelings of failure and wanting to give up before you've even properly started.

I want to encourage you to see mindfulness not as a duty, or a drudge, but as a wonderful, life-affirming opportunity. Definitely not something that you *have to do*, or *ought to do*, but something that you *want to do*, that you *get the opportunity to do*. And I believe that this is possible if 1) you start small and build on that, 2) you understand the difference between formal and informal mindfulness practice so that you can gradually incorporate mindfulness into the whole of your daily life, from studying to eating, from walking to conversations with friends, and 3) have a clear and realistic intention for practising mindfulness.

Let's start by looking at formal mindfulness practice.

FORMAL MINDFULNESS PRACTICE

When we talk about mindfulness, people usually think about meditation. However, it's important to realise that meditation is only one way of practising mindfulness. For sure, an important way, the foundation for a life-enhancing practice, but it is just one aspect of mindfulness. And what is meditation? It comprises:

- adopting a body posture that encourages alertness, concentration and awareness;
- consciously and deliberately choosing an object to focus on for a set period of time – usually, this 'object' is your breath, but it can also be other things such as sounds, bodily sensations, a mantra or your flow of thoughts;
- bringing your awareness to the object of your focus and holding it there gently;
- bringing your awareness back to the object of your focus whenever you realise that your concentration has wandered.

That last point is crucial. Wandering attention is not a sign that you can't meditate, or that you're not trying hard enough. This is what happens to everyone – from the Zen master, right down to you – sitting on your chair in your student house or halls of residence. Our minds wander, constantly. And that's OK. For however long we have decided we will meditate, we bring our attention back to our breath, or to sounds, over and over again. This is meditation.

Meditation is *not*:

- clearing or emptying your mind;
- having blissful experiences (these may happen from time to time, but are definitely not to be chased, or used as a way of judging your meditation practice).

As I've said already: mindfulness is simple, but not easy.

Let's try it: something simple.

MINDFUL EXERCISE

Find yourself a quiet spot – in a library, on a park bench, in your bedroom. Somewhere you won't be disturbed.

Put your phone away: preferably turn it off, but at least put it onto silent/ flight mode. Don't be tempted to use it as a timer unless you switch off all incoming alerts. You'll see messages coming through that will distract you.

Sit as comfortably as you can on a supportive chair: feet flat on the floor; back upright but not stiff; your head tilted very slightly down; hands resting on your thighs or knees. If you want to sit cross-legged on the floor, that's fine; but it's also fine to sit on a chair – preferably one that isn't so comfortable that you simply fall asleep.

Take a moment to 'arrive': just settle in for a minute. Simply be aware of sitting here. Taking some nice slow deep breaths helps to relax the body and mind. As you breathe out, let go of tension, stress and worry.

Let yourself become aware of the space around you: the height of the room, colours you can see, any scents or sounds, the quality of the light. Just noticing, not making a story with it.

Be aware when your attention wanders away to other things. For example, what you were doing earlier today/yesterday; what you plan to do later; worries or concerns that are around at the moment. Just notice your wandering mind, and gently, and without criticism, refocus on the space around you for a few more moments.

Now, on an out-breath, gently close your eyes. (It's also OK to keep your eyes open if you think you might fall asleep, or if you just prefer it that way – simply lower your gaze to a spot on the floor a few feet in front of you.) Tune in to the sensation of breath in your body. Don't try to force it, or make your breathing exaggerated. Simply begin to notice something that is happening all the time but that you rarely acknowledge: you are

● ● ● ●

breathing. A gentle rise and fall of your chest and stomach, air entering your body through your nose or mouth, and then – as your body lets go – flowing back out into the space around you.

You can put a hand on your chest and stomach if you like, so that you get a sense of where in the body your breathing is most vivid.

Now start to count your breaths. Breathe in, one. Breathe out, one. Breathe in, two. Breathe out, two. Keep going like this all the way up to ten. Don't force or change your breathing; keep it as natural as you can.

When you reach ten, start to count backwards: Breathe in, ten. Breathe out, ten. Breathe in, nine. Breathe out, nine. All the way back to one.

When (not if) your attention wanders and you lose count, start over. Go back to counting from one. Don't try to guess or remember where you'd got to. Just gently, and without criticising yourself, start again.

When you do get back to one, or when your time is up, just sit for another minute and tune in to the feeling of you, sitting here, breathing. Not trying to achieve anything, get anywhere, or feel anything special.

Then, simply open your eyes or lift your gaze and gently move on with whatever needs doing next.

LISTEN TO THE AUDIO CLIP AT
https://study.sagepub.com/mindfulness

This is a gentle, simple formal mindfulness practice. Formal, because you stop whatever you were doing and make a deliberate effort to devote yourself – for however long you choose – to meditate, to be present with yourself, to develop concentration and to being in the moment. You commit to *falling awake*, rather than falling asleep or continuing in the automatic thought and feeling patterns that tend to dominate our waking hours.

Formal practice is undoubtedly a commitment. But it doesn't need to be onerous – and certainly nothing like the fifty-minute exercise I was given in my first mindfulness course. It is better to practise regularly for five or ten minutes – every day if possible, but hopefully not fewer than three times a week – than trying to do too much and give up, or only achieve it irregularly. To some dedicated meditators, five or ten minutes may sound like nothing, but I am a firm believer in starting small and building on whatever emerges from the seeds that are planted. Eventually, you can build up to longer mindfulness meditation sessions – perhaps at weekends, or during vacations. The important thing is to keep going. However, be realistic. Don't aim for twenty minutes a day if this is completely unrealistic: five minutes is fine. You can build on this.

VARIATIONS ON THE BASIC PRACTICE

After several weeks of the practice described above, start to count only the out-breath rather than the in-breath as well. And again, if/when you lose count, just start again. Don't worry: you are not in a competition. No one is judging you. It's OK to start again, over and over, and it's completely normal.

Then, after several more weeks, stop counting and allow your focus to simply be on your breath. Gently stay with the sensation of breathing for however long you have decided to practise – again, bringing your attention back when it wanders, as it surely will.

After several weeks of using the breath as your focus for meditation, change the focus of your attention to sounds. As you sit on your chair, tune in to sounds as they come and go. Subtle sounds like air-conditioning or distant traffic, or obvious sounds like people talking or music. Notice the gaps between sounds. Notice any tendency to create stories about the sounds and what they mean – to label some sounds as 'nice' and others as 'bad'. Try to stay simply with the sound itself, noticing the stories your mind tends to create – and then letting those stories go.

A nice way to practise formal meditation is as follows:

MINDFUL EXERCISE

Decide how long you will practise for: anything up to thirty minutes is great. Turn off all distracting devices: anything that beeps. Get into your comfortable sitting position – on your chair or cross-legged on the floor, or on a meditation stool or mat.

- Take a moment to settle: simply 'arrive' where you are – notice your body as fully as possible – any tension or aches, or simply no particular feeling at all.

- Take several nice slow deep breaths, letting go of any tension or anxiety as you breathe out. Do this for a minute or so.

- Then close your eyes, if you choose, or lower your gaze to the floor.

- Bring your attention to any sounds that are around you, and keep your focus on sounds for about one third of the time you are setting aside to meditate. Let sounds be your focus: coming and going, pleasant and unpleasant, loud, gentle, subtle.

- Then change the focus of your attention to your breath: tune in to the sensation of breathing in your body, noticing where it is most 'alive' – in your chest or stomach. Either count your breaths, or let go of the counting and simply focus on the sensation itself. Do this for another third of the time you have set aside.

- And then for the final third of the time you have set aside, allow your focus to go where it wants to go – and gently notice it as it shifts. Perhaps it goes back to sounds, or to your breath; or perhaps you notice that you are focusing on thoughts or emotions. Just notice the

● ● ● ●

subtle change in focus: a kind of choiceless awareness of where your mind chooses to go to.

- Finally, open your eyes if they were closed, or lift your gaze. Take a few more deep breaths, and then slowly and mindfully stand up and move gently onto whatever comes next in your day.

Another way to practise formal mindfulness is to do some walking meditation. This is particularly helpful if you find that your mind is very agitated or restless, and that sitting meditation is simply too much for you for a while. You can also do walking meditation if sitting meditation is not recommended for you (as, for example, if you are dealing with acute anxiety or depression – see Chapter 1 for other conditions where formal mindfulness may be unhelpful). In walking meditation, we are deliberately switching the focus of our attention to the physical sensations of walking: the feel of our feet on the floor, the lifting of our feet and legs as we walk slowly along the space we are in, noticing the way our bodies sway and move as we try to keep our balance. Just noticing something that, most of the time, we do on autopilot as we move from one place to another without even being conscious of the amazing way we move our bodies and stay upright.

There are two ways to practise walking meditation:

1. Slow walking meditation requires a reasonable space in which to walk up and down: if your room is large enough, that will be fine. Otherwise, you could go to the park, or find somewhere like a chaplaincy on campus and ask if you can use a room there. Bring your full attention to each tiny

● ● ● ●

movement of your feet, your legs, your arms – the rest of your body – as you very slowly and deliberately walk around the space you are in. Use the sensations of your body as your focus for your practice. This is walking – but not in the way that you are probably used to it.

2. Although some forms of walking meditation involve slowing down to such an extent that you could only practise in a specific space away from outside distractions, it is also a beautiful experience if you are lucky enough to find a quiet, attractive space such as a wood or park where you might only slow your pace down very slightly from your usual walking speed. It can also be very rewarding even if you are doing something as mundane as walking between lectures or walking home at the end of the day. Instead of getting lost in your music, come into the present by the means of walking meditation, your focus resting gently on the physical sensations throughout your body as you walk. You can also tune in to sounds, sights, aromas – diving into the sensual experience of walking as deeply as possible. As usual, whenever your mind wanders – worrying, fantasising, planning – notice this, and then refocus on walking until you reach your destination. No more arriving somewhere and wondering how on earth you got there because your mind was elsewhere.

INFORMAL MINDFULNESS PRACTICE

Having looked at what formal mindfulness practice might look like, we can now begin to consider what *informal* practice is, and how you can incorporate it into more and more aspects of your daily life as a student. You might be wondering: 'Why would I want to do that?' I suppose the fundamental answer is: the more of your life that you are aware of, the more you can bring gentle awareness to your daily activities, the less space there is for anxiety and depression, perfectionism and impostor syndrome to take over your experience. So often, we spend much of our days caught up in the working of the reptilian brain (fight, flight or freeze) or the limbic brain (intense emotions, upsetting memories) that the reality of life is simply squeezed out. By deliberately practising mindfulness throughout the day, we 'wake up' from the trance of our habitual thoughts and behaviour patterns and notice more of what is happening right here, right now.

Basically, there is no part of your life to which you cannot bring mindfulness; for example, washing, cleaning, cooking, shopping, eating, talking, listening, playing sport, taking exams and making presentations. Every activity you are involved in can be done mindfully, or mindlessly: mindfully, by bringing gentle, compassionate attention to your experience, whether it is enjoyable or not, painful or not; mindlessly, by ignoring your physical experience, but instead being tossed around on the never-ending stream of thoughts, images and behaviours produced by your always-active monkey mind.

A MINDFUL SHOWER

I remember one mindfulness teacher telling me that she suddenly realised that she was sharing her shower with her boss nearly every morning! I wondered what on earth she meant, at first. Then she explained that too often, rather than simply being in the shower – feeling the warm water, smelling the soap and shampoo, hearing the water gurgling away down the drain – she was caught up in arguments and conflicts with her boss at work. This was a very good example of how bringing mindfulness to an ordinary, everyday activity can transform that experience. It takes practice and determination *not* to invite someone 'into the shower' with you. One aspect of human nature is that we quite enjoy being angry with someone, or replaying an argument, or imagining what we'll tell them next time they dare cross our paths. It's juicy and adrenalin flows; it's quite addictive, this soap-opera existence in the mind. If we're not careful, we can waste most of our lives in a drama of our own creation – meanwhile, the beautiful luxury of a warm shower has completely passed us by.

Here are some activities you could bring mindful attention to, and notice whenever your attention has swung off into the soap opera that your mind can so easily create for you:

- *Brushing your teeth*: a perfect opportunity to be fully present for three or four minutes, tasting the toothpaste, feeling the brush, hearing the water.
- *Washing up*: for many, a chore to be avoided, but, with mindful intention, a wonderful chance to feel the warm water in the bowl, focus on each dish so that it is as clean as it can be, manipulate the brush or mop, stack the dishes carefully so that they don't slip or crash against each other.
- *Sitting in a lecture*: perhaps you like to write shopping lists in lectures, or send messages on your phone. Try being fully present instead: tune into the space you are sitting in, notice the colours, sounds, scents around you, notice when your mind produces unhelpful thoughts for you such as 'I don't understand this at all', 'This is boring', 'This lecturer is useless'. See them as distractions from your simple task of being a student, attending a lecture, taking notes as best you can.
- *Cooking*: chopping an onion is a wonderful opportunity to practise mindfulness. The feel of the knife in your hand, the subtle movements needed to chop the onion safely, the sound of the onion being chopped, the tears that emerge from your eyes! Try not to rush food preparation. Instead, bring your full attention to it; notice the textures, the colours, the scents, the tastes.
- *Eating*: how often do you wolf something down without even really tasting it? A bag of crisps, biscuits, a sandwich – they can all go down the hatch in seconds without you having even noticed that you had consumed them. Try eating a sandwich mindfully, or an apple. Instead of eating while doing something else (put that phone down), make your food the sole focus of your attention. Sense the texture in your hand – is it soft? Smooth? Rough? Hard? The scent – is it spicy? Sweet? Strong? Undetectable? The taste – is it sweet? Sour? Salty? Pay attention to the feel in your mouth; notice your jaw as it chews, your tongue as it moves around inside your mouth. Notice, when you swallow, the saliva produced in your mouth before, during and after you eat. The seemingly ordinary activity of eating pizza is actually a miraculous combination of experiences that are all too often missed.

The list of informal mindfulness practices could go on indefinitely. Think about your own life. What activities might you bring a mindful presence to? And how might that enrich your experience of those activities?

THE IMPORTANCE OF INTENTION

It's all very well having a go at formal and informal mindfulness practice. But, without a motivation for continuing to practice, the reality is that you are unlikely to commit to the kind of practice that will bear fruit in terms of greater clarity of thinking and a richer, more nuanced experience of life around you.

Think back to Greg, the harassed physics student we met at the start of this chapter. With the amount of work he has to do, what will motivate him to carve out some time in his schedule to practise mindfulness? As with any activity, if we are not clear about why we are doing it, we are unlikely to keep at it for long, especially when inevitable challenges arise.

It's important that you take some time before you start any mindfulness practice to ask yourself why this is important for you, and to check that your reasons are realistic. I'm going to suggest some reasons for practising mindfulness that may help you, and also point out those that I am sure will not.

Helpful reasons for practising mindfulness:

- to wake up from the trance of your automatic thoughts, many of which are unhelpful but can dominate your life;
- to experience your life more fully without the usual worries, regrets, anxieties and fears getting in the way;
- to experience *being* rather than *doing* – to come to an awareness that you are not just your thoughts;
- to develop confidence in your ability to take refuge in your body, breath, sounds and sights when thoughts and emotions bother and torment you.

Unhelpful (unrealistic) reasons for practising mindfulness:

- to never feel bothered by life's circumstances again;
- to have a peaceful, tranquil mind at all times;
- to feel special emotions or have ecstatic experiences;
- to escape from the problems you have in your life.

BUILDING YOUR OWN MINDFULNESS PRACTICE

You will now have a clearer understanding of the difference between formal and informal mindfulness practice. One last important point to understand is that formal practice is the foundation for informal practice. In other words, you can't simply have mindful showers every day and generate the kind of awareness that will genuinely make a difference in your life. Why? Well, because, as we saw in Chapter 2, our monkey minds are powerful, instinctive organisms and we really do need some clearly defined time in which we consciously decide to sit and focus away from those habitual patterns. In formal practice, we are developing an ability to make a decision to stay with our practice, whatever monkey mind is up to – to strengthen our powers of concentration and awareness. Some days you may be quite quiet and calm, and on others you may feel that your ability to focus can be measured in milliseconds. What counts is that you 'keep on keeping on', developing your ability to recognise thoughts as *just* thoughts rather than commands to be obeyed, or truths that cannot be questioned. Formal practice gives you the space and time to experience the good, the bad and the ugly of your mind, without judgement or self-condemnation. This is why it is so important.

Of course, Greg would tell us that he has no time for formal practice and you may feel the same. But remember: we are not looking at an unrealistic, unattainable period of time sitting on your meditation cushion. To begin with, Greg could decide to practise formal mindfulness meditation for just ten minutes, three times a week. Quite simply, if you tell yourself you don't have that amount of time, you are fooling yourself. We all find time to watch TV, to surf the net, to listen to music. So let's be real: if you truly want to explore

mindfulness, it takes commitment. It is not a quick fix; you are planting seeds that may take many weeks and months to grow. But if you keep at it, the results will begin to show in your life – your practice is its own reward.

Let's now have a look at an example of how a basic practice might look:

Monday: Ten minutes sitting meditation (best early in the morning).

Mindful walking to and from campus (no headphones, just tuning in to whatever is going on around you).

One other mindful activity – for example, a shower or a lunch.

Tuesday: Mindful walking to and from campus.

Wednesday: Mindful walking plus another activity, such as listening to music without distractions, reading a short passage from a book about mindfulness.

Thursday: Ten minutes sitting meditation.

Mindful walking.

Friday: Mindful walking and mindful lunch.

Saturday: Twenty minutes sitting meditation.

Mindful eating and walking.

Sunday: Day off, including a digital detox for morning, afternoon or evening – just relaxing and reflecting on what it has been like to practise mindfulness this week. What did you notice? When did it feel OK? When did you give up? Were you being too hard on yourself (very common)? Did you give up too easily as soon as you felt boredom or irritation? What changes, if any, do you want to make in the coming week?

You can add extra time to the formal practice sessions whenever you like, and I hope that you will discover the real benefits of longer periods of practice. But remember that it is better to practise for ten minutes three times a week than thirty minutes once. Keep your formal

Mindfulness: Formal and Informal   47

practice short but regular. Use guided mindfulness meditations if they help (see suggested sources in the Afterword) or, if one is available, join a mindfulness group on campus and practise with other people. This can be a really helpful thing to do, as long as the practice being taught is realistic and not overly demanding: beware fifty-minute body-scans.

Remember, we are looking for the *middle way* through the temptations of mindfulness extremism (where only long, intense, formal practice is seen as having value) and mindfulness self-delusion (where five minutes of half-heartedly trying to be mindful while watching TV gets you absolutely nowhere). Effort *is* required, but so is self-compassion. Your task is to experiment, explore and find the right balance for you.

QUESTIONS FOR REFLECTION

1. Take some time to think about your motivation for wanting to explore mindfulness. What are you hoping may emerge from this? Using the material from this chapter, can you gauge whether any of these hopes may be unrealistic and unhelpful?

2. Formal mindfulness is the foundation for informal practice. How much time do you realistically want to set aside for this each week? Can you make a real commitment to these periods of time? What might prevent you from keeping to your plan? And how might you cope with those obstacles?

3. It's a good idea, each time you sit to practise formal mindfulness meditation, to remind yourself of your intention for sitting. Can you write one simple, clear sentence to express your intention for sitting in mindfulness meditation? (It's fine for this to evolve as your practice deepens, but you will find it helpful to keep your intention in mind each time you come to sit.)

FURTHER READING

Jack Kornfield (2008). *Meditation for Beginners*. London: Bantam.

Gentle and clear guidance about how to build a meditation practice. The author offers guidance about overcoming typical obstacles to the commitment required.

Laurie J. Cameron (2018). *The Mindful Day: Practical Ways To Find Focus, Calm And Joy From Morning To Evening*. National Geographic.

The author shows how ordinary activity can be transformed by the practice of mindfulness. She outlines simple ways to incorporate mindfulness throughout your day.

REFERENCES

Davidson, J. (2016). How long does it take to become enlightened? Available at: https://jessicadavidson.co.uk/2016/03/04/how-long-does-it-take-to-become-enlightened/ (accessed 16 January 2019).

Thich Nhat Hanh (2017) *The Art of Living*. New York, NY: HarperCollins.

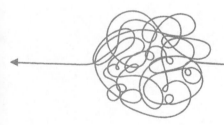

'...YOU ARE ONLY BEING ASKED TO

RELAX, ALLOW LIFE
TO BE AS IT IS,
AND OPEN YOUR HEART

TO YOURSELF. IT'S EASIER THAN YOU MIGHT
THINK, AND IT COULD CHANGE YOUR LIFE.,

Kristin Neff,
Self-compassion (2011)

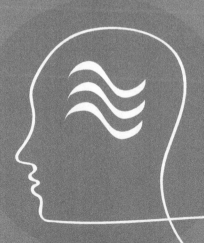

4

MINDFULNESS ᴬᴺᴰ SELF-COMPASSION

IN THIS CHAPTER YOU WILL:

- explore why compassion, for self and others, is at the heart of mindfulness practice;

- understand the social and cultural pressures that militate against developing self-compassion;

- comprehend how mindfulness can help you to consciously cultivate self and other-compassion;

- discover how self-compassion can transform the way you relate to your own human vulnerability.

Charles is dogged by a constant feeling of imminent disaster. It's as if he's waiting for the tap on the shoulder that will signal that something awful has happened such as he's being kicked off his course, his girlfriend has dumped him or his housemates want him to move out. For as long as he can remember, Charles has never felt that he quite measures up, that other people are somehow 'better' than he is. Charles has high-achieving parents and siblings. His dad is a lawyer and his mum a GP. His sister is at Cambridge and Charles desperately hoped that he would be able to follow in her footsteps but didn't get the grades he needed. In his relationships with friends, housemates and girlfriend, Charles is always trying to please – to second-guess what others want, rather than saying what he wants. A typical response to any question that involves expressing an opinion or a preference is: 'I don't mind. What would you like to do?' Deep down, Charles is extremely self-critical. He doesn't like the way he looks, he thinks he is too short; when he struggles to understand new ideas on his course, he tells himself that he's stupid; at night in bed, he replays conversations he's had during the day, thinking about what he said, what he should have said, and how other people must think he's boring or offensive. Currently, Charles is aiming to run a marathon in the summer vacation, and gets up at 6.30 am every day to go for a run. Unsurprisingly, he tends to think that he is not doing very well, that he should try harder, and that other people clearly find doing something like this much easier.

WHY SELF-COMPASSION IS HARD

'Try harder!'

'No pain – no gain.'

'Push yourself.'

'Lunch is for wimps.'

Pressure, pressure, pressure. We live in a pressurised world where we are urged to push ourselves hard, achieve great things and not to feel or display vulnerability. There is pressure to get good grades at school, then at university. There is pressure to get a good job, to have a great relationship, to make the most of ourselves. From an early age, we receive messages that it is not OK to be satisfied with the status quo: we must always be striving to do more, be more, achieve more. Not surprisingly, many of us can end up feeling like failures. It seems we are biologically programmed to compare ourselves 'upwards' – that is, to compare ourselves to those people we think are doing just a little better than we are (slightly better looking, getting grades that are just above ours, earning slightly more money than us), and as a result end up feeling a constant, low-grade dissatisfaction with ourselves and with life. It's interesting that we tend not to compare 'downwards' with those who are less fortunate than we are; it's those who are just a little above us who we use to benchmark our own existence (de Botton, 2005).

Therefore, inside all of us there is a little voice that nags at us, undermining our contentment and peace of mind. Either we berate *ourselves* – 'I must try harder', 'Why can't I be as clever/attractive/funny as him/her?' – or we condemn *others* – 'They're such a pain, always flaunting their success', 'I'd love him to fall flat on his face and look like an idiot', 'I can never forgive him/her for what she said/did'. It seems that as a culture, we think that 'big stick' beats 'carrot' every time when it comes to how to motivate ourselves: we think that if we are hard on ourselves (and others), we will achieve more. I've seen many students in counselling sessions who sincerely tell me that unless they are tough on themselves, criticise themselves, bully themselves, they won't achieve anything. They think that if they are kinder, more understanding towards themselves, they will simply end up lounging around all day doing nothing.

It's interesting how we seem to have a tendency to be either *hard* or *soft* on ourselves (Barker, 2018). We seem to think that we must either push ourselves almost to the brink of physical exhaustion, or, alternatively, give up. So we tend to say things like: 'I'm going to do ten hours work in the library every day next week' (hard) or 'I just couldn't be bothered, so I stayed in bed all morning' (soft). It's all-or-nothing thinking: push myself, beat myself over the head with criticism, or just give up.

Neither the hard nor the soft approach to life works in our interests. One of the key drivers in certain eating disorders is precisely this *hard* (starve myself all day) and *soft* (have a cereal/biscuit binge) dynamic: one follows the other as night follows day. Try too hard, then give up; then pull myself together and try hard again; then give up – and so on. We need a better way to relate to ourselves and to our lives.

WHAT IS SELF-COMPASSION?

Imagine that you meet a child, about seven or eight years old. They are really upset and tell you that they hate themselves because they can't do their homework like everyone else and they don't have any friends at school. What would your reaction be to this child? Would you shout at them and tell them to pull themselves together? Tell them to stop making pathetic excuses and just get on with it? I'm hoping not. Most people, seeing a distressed child, want to reassure them, to encourage them, to help them. This is at the heart of self-compassion: an ability to relate to our own vulnerability with the same care, attention and encouragement that we would offer to a small child. The reality is that life presents us with challenges that test our abilities and lead us to make mistakes of many kinds. None of us is perfect. We are all comparing ourselves upwards and often feel somehow inadequate because of the thoughts our minds generate based on these comparisons. Table 4.1 shows some examples of how our 'hard', critical voice can undermine us, how our 'soft', helpless voice can leave us paralysed, and how a more self-compassionate voice doesn't ignore the anxiety or fear, but nevertheless encourages us to take meaningful action.

SITUATION	CRITICAL VOICE	HELPLESS VOICE	SELF-COMPASSIONATE VOICE
ASKING A QUESTION IN A SEMINAR ▶▶▶	I'll look like such an idiot if I ask a question. Everyone, including the tutor, will think I'm a total moron. Everyone else knows what they're talking about. I daren't open my mouth because I'll just reveal how ignorant I am.	I won't ask a question in seminars. That way I'll stay safe and avoid feeling anxious.	This is a hard thing to do. I can feel my anxiety rising at the thought of it. But probably most people feel anxious about this. My anxiety is not unusual. I can ask a simple question to start with and build on that. It's OK to feel anxious. I'm not an idiot, I'm simply a vulnerable human being.
SITTING AN EXAM ▶▶▶▶▶	When I turn the paper over, I should know the answers to all the questions. I have to feel calm and confident like everyone else. Other people don't feel the way I do, so I must not feel anxious.	Exams are too hard for me. If I feel at all anxious, I tell myself I'm having a panic attack which makes things worse, so I try everything I can to avoid exams. I can only contemplate exams if I get 'special conditions' for taking them.	It's not unusual to feel anxiety around exams. Everyone does. That's normal. I won't beat myself up for that. This is a demanding situation. I will do as well as I can and remind myself that everyone in the room is feeling anxiety too. It's normal; I'm normal.
ASKING SOMEONE OUT ON A DATE ▶▶▶▶▶	If I ask someone on a date, they have to accept, or I can't stand it. I have to be successful when dating and I must always have someone who other people consider 'attractive' to go out with.	Asking someone on a date is way too scary for me. I'd never do it. Anyone I like would never like me back, and I can't cope with rejection. I'll just stay in and watch some box sets.	Taking the step of asking someone out is kind of scary. I'm revealing something about myself which is very personal and I could get hurt here. This isn't easy – and it's not easy for anyone. It's OK to feel scared and it's OK to feel upset if I get rejected. But I can handle this. It's not easy but I can handle it.

Table 4.1   Self-talk and self-compassion

MINDFUL EXERCISE

Take a moment now to think about a situation or a relationship that you find difficult. Best to think of something or someone that isn't too difficult. Perhaps a topic you're struggling with slightly on your course, or a good friend you recently had a bit of a falling out with. You can keep really difficult situations for later, after you become more practised at expressing compassion rather than criticism.

Look back at Table 4.1 and write down a brief description of the situation you have brought to mind. Then write down whatever 'hard' thoughts you have about this situation/relationship. 'I'm such an idiot, everyone else understands this subject. I'm never going to get on top of this.'

Now, write down the 'soft' thoughts you have about this situation/relationship (usually characterised by a plan to *avoid* the difficulty you are facing): 'I'm such rubbish at getting on with people, I'll just keep out of everyone's way. It's so much easier not to bother with people.'

Now, take some time to write down a more compassionate response to whatever hard/soft thoughts you came up with. If it helps, imagine that you are responding to a friend, or a young child, who has told you about this situation. What can you say to them/yourself? 'Yes, it's hard, isn't it? But don't give up. Take your time. Ask for help if you need it and try not to let imagined thoughts about what other people think or feel get you down.' 'Don't forget that most people struggle with things like this. There's nothing wrong with you. You don't need to beat yourself up over this.'

If you can, practise this exercise once a day for two weeks, using different situations, so that you really begin to get the idea that compassionate, understanding self-talk can make a deep difference to how you cope with the challenges of life.

Self-compassion is: acknowledging our vulnerabilities without criticism on the basis that what each of us feels in a given situation is similar to what others feel. Allowing ourselves to know our vulnerabilities deeply and intimately (our fears, our insecurities,

our anxieties) and actively encouraging ourselves in the face of those vulnerabilities *as we would a small child who felt the same way.*

Self-compassion is not: self-pity. Self-compassion is not the 'soft' voice that lets us off the hook of challenge, or that says 'It doesn't matter: you can't be expected to sit that exam/ask a question when you feel like this'. And neither is it the voice that tells us we must always feel happy and comfortable: it is not self-indulgence.

Developing self-compassion may not be easy to do if you have internalised messages from culture, family or friends that you are somehow defective, that you must not reveal your vulnerabilities, or that you should always be striving to achieve more. If you have been bullied at school, or at university itself, if you have suffered any kind of abuse (physical, sexual, emotional) or if you have grown up in a family where high emphasis has been placed on achievement, you may need help in learning to develop the kind of self-compassion that can free you up to relax with yourself and life just-as-it-is. Life is never perfect and neither are we. Being a human being in our complex, demanding world is not easy. We all need self-compassion to help us relax in life, accepting our less-than-perfect existence.

HOW CAN MINDFULNESS HELP ME DEVELOP SELF-COMPASSION?

One of the key aims of mindfulness practice is the development of self-compassion. The Sanskrit word '*maitri*' (meaning 'kindness', 'friendliness', 'benevolence') is found in many Buddhist texts and emphasises the centrality of this stance towards ourselves as we engage in mindfulness. Without this stance, we are very likely to give up any formal practice of meditation. We will simply become exasperated with ourselves as we notice how much our mind wanders whenever we sit to practise; how violent, sexual and downright weird our thoughts can be, very far removed from our hopes of sitting in blissful peace. Meditators can be far too hard on themselves as they strive for enlightenment. 'Upward comparison' creeps in so easily. We tell ourselves we should be sitting for longer; that our minds should not be wandering so much; that we should be having the kinds of blissful experiences we sometimes hear that others have had. Tara Brach, an American psychotherapist and mindfulness teacher, suggests that there are two 'wings' to the 'bird' of what she terms 'Radical Acceptance' – an ability to gently engage with life just-as-it-is: mindfulness and compassion. If we only have mindfulness, we may find that what we discover about ourselves is hard to bear; the kind of thoughts and emotions generated by our reptilian brain (remember the four Fs we looked at in Chapter 2?) may be highly anxious, violent, sexual, covetous. Through mindfulness we generate awareness of our thoughts and feelings, and an ability to observe them rather than simply becoming enmeshed with them. With the addition of compassion, we avoid the harsh self-and-other criticism that might otherwise arise. As Brach writes: 'When the two wings of Radical Acceptance, mindfulness and compassion, are present, our relationships with others become a sacred vessel for spiritual freedom' (Brach, 2003).

The reality is that mindfulness meditation is often a very ordinary experience and the truth is that we may not like that. We would prefer it to be exhilarating, special, extraordinary. We may tell ourselves, 'I'm too stressed to practise mindfulness now' or 'I feel too down to practise mindfulness'. This is our monkey mind trying to convince us that we can only practise mindfulness when we feel calm, clear, centred. This pretty much rules out 95 per cent of the time for most of us. Therefore, any commitment to formal mindfulness practice of necessity depends on an attitude of self-compassion: 'This is not easy; in fact, this is quite hard. I often feel like giving up, or skipping a session. Sometimes it feels really boring to sit and meditate. That's OK. That's normal. Other people feel the same way too. All I have to do is show up, keep going, and not worry about how my mind tells me things *should* be.'

A crucial element in the development of self-compassion is the ability – beautifully fostered by formal mindful practice – to notice the hard, self-bullying thoughts that arise in our minds *about our mindfulness practice*. 'I'm rubbish at this.' 'This is useless; what's the point?' 'Other people can do this, but not me.' 'This is so boring! I'm obviously doing this wrong: there must be more to it than this.' 'I should be practising much longer than I am. What use is ten minutes?' The scouts have a motto: 'Be prepared!' We must 'be prepared' for these hard, self-critical thoughts that will definitely arise when we try to get serious about formal mindfulness practice. Being prepared, not being taken by surprise when these thoughts appear, can begin to rob them of their power to undermine us and deflect us from engaging in something that has meaning for us.

As you develop mindful self-compassion about the thoughts your mind produces towards your formal practice, you will begin to be able to carry this awareness into more and more of your life. You will become better at detecting the undermining thoughts that your mind produces in other situations, and understand that these thoughts are usually, habitual, repetitive 'mental events' (Williams and Penman, 2011) rather than 'the truth'. You will begin to experience emotional freedom.

I recently sat down to meditate for a while with the intention simply of allowing myself to take time out from a busy schedule and to experience some moments of stillness. Almost as soon as I started to meditate, I became plagued by the thought: 'I should get a new phone.' And then: 'I wonder if I'm entitled to an upgrade yet?' And then: 'I'd really like a new phone – I think the new ones make emojis from your own face.' It took me several moments to 'come to' and realise that I had almost immediately become lost in a fantasy about a new mobile phone – something that I don't need, don't particularly want, but that I could otherwise have spent hours fantasising about. I was able to gently give these thoughts a label: 'wanting' and then return to focusing on my breath. Within moments, my mind took off down another pathway, this time thinking about Christmas cards and whether I should send one to someone I didn't hear from last year: 'worrying'. Back to my breath. And so on. It's so important that I didn't start berating myself with criticism: 'I can't do this: I'm useless at meditating.' Instead, I simply acknowledged that I am no different from anyone else: my mind wanders around all over the place, worrying and remembering, wanting and fantasising. 'It's OK, this isn't easy. You're doing OK, keep going.' It's a much more helpful way to respond than, 'Oh I give up. Let's just go and check my mobile phone contract.'

MINDFUL EXERCISE

Developing self-compassion is fundamental to cultivating mindfulness. As we've seen, without compassion, mindfulness can feel too harshly revealing of our human frailties and vulnerabilities.

Take some time to sit in formal mindfulness practice. Fifteen minutes is good for this exercise. You need some time to settle, and then some more time to engage in the meditation itself.

To start with, turn your phone off and make yourself comfortable. Meditation should not be about sitting in uncomfortable positions, or forcing your body to adopt a posture that is not 'right' for you. Find a chair, a cushion, a mat – whatever works for you. For a couple of minutes, bring your awareness to simply sitting here, to the weight of your body pressing down, then to any physical sensations you notice in your body, and then to sights and sounds around you. When your mind wanders, simply notice this, and gently bring your attention back to your body and the space around you.

Now take some slow, deep breaths – make the out-breath slightly longer than the in-breath. As you breathe out, let go of any tension you feel in your body: in your face, your shoulders, your arms, your stomach, your legs. Slow, deep breaths. Letting go of worries and concerns for the next few moments.

Now, slowly read or repeat these sentences to yourself (if you are reading, obviously keep your eyes open, or if you are repeating from the recording,

● ● ● ●

you can close your eyes). Let the words sink in. Wait for thirty seconds between sentences, noticing how your mind and body react to them. There is no right way to react – just noticing, bringing mindfulness and awareness to your reactions.

- Today, as I think about myself and my life, I accept that I am a vulnerable, fallible human being.

- I let go of striving for perfection.

- I acknowledge that fear and sadness are part of being human.

- I forgive myself for being hard on myself.

- I intend to be gentle with myself and to encourage myself when difficult feelings arise.

- I intend to accept myself just as I am.

- I intend to let go of harsh self-criticism.

- I intend to be as kind to myself as I would be to anyone else.

- Today, as I think about the other people in my life and who live around me, I accept that everyone is a vulnerable, fallible human being.

- I let go of expecting perfection in others.

- I acknowledge that the fears and sadness I feel are shared by everyone.

- I forgive others for letting me down or hurting me.

- I intend to be kind to others and to encourage those who are struggling.

- I accept others as I find them, not as I think they should be.

- I let go of criticising others.

- I wish everyone at least some degree of peace and happiness.

Now, sit quietly for a while and notice your reactions to these sentences. Is there any sense of peace? Or irritation? Comfort? Disbelief? Was it easier to be kind to yourself, or to others? Or the other way round? Just notice your reactions. That's all you have to do.

Then allow yourself to take a few more slow deep breaths. If you have closed your eyes, gently open them, and come back into the space around you.

To end, choose one of these sentences. Maybe write it down on a card somewhere you'll see it often during the day and let it be a reminder throughout the next twenty-four hours of your intention to cultivate compassion within yourself.

And then gently move on to whatever comes next in your day.

LISTEN TO THE AUDIO CLIP AT
https://study.sagepub.com/mindfulness

When Charles began to practise compassion, he found it much easier to be compassionate towards others than to himself. He became aware that he was much more understanding of others' mistakes and failings than of his own. This, in itself, was new awareness for Charles. Very slowly, over several months, Charles began to be able to see how being so hard on himself was not helping him. In fact, it was just making life miserable. One of the hardest things for him to accept and be understanding about was his height. He recognised an intense longing to be tall. He recognised a deep sadness within him that he would never be tall. And he started to acknowledge that he was not the only person who might wish they were taller. In fact, he started to notice that some other men were quite a bit shorter than he was. He began to talk more compassionately to himself: 'Yes, it's a big

disappointment that I'll never be 6ft tall. It's something I would have loved for myself. It's hard for me. And I also recognise that many other people worry about the way they look; most people are unhappy about something to do with their physical appearance. I can't change my height. But I can remember that most other people are more interested in themselves rather than other people, and my height may not be such a big issue for others. In fact, they may not even notice it. When I feel self-conscious about my height, I'll remind myself that I do have other positive qualities, such as my sense of humour, and that feeling vulnerable about physical appearance is a normal part of being human.'

Did being more compassionate make Charles taller? Of course not. The wish that he could be taller may always stay with him. However, he is starting to be able to accept this wish, and not to beat himself up for it. He can recognise that his vulnerability is not his alone, but something shared by most people. He is beginning to be self-and-other compassionate.

COMPASSION FOR SELF – AND OTHERS

This last point is crucial too: mindfulness helps us to see and accept our own foibles and vulnerabilities. It should also help us to understand other people when they are behaving 'badly' or 'madly'. Vulnerability is never far below the surface for any of us, and can often help us to understand difficult people. Anger, for example, is simply the tip of an iceberg, the part that is visible above the waterline: underneath, usually, are the much bigger, more sensitive, hidden emotions of hurt or fear. Revealing hurt and fear is potentially a scary thing to do because we might get ridiculed or ignored, which would make things even worse. It's perhaps simpler to attack someone else through anger than to acknowledge our own vulnerability.

Many students, especially in their first year away from home, experience high levels of anxiety, but may try to cover it up by getting very drunk, being over-confident and loud, or shutting themselves away in their rooms and rarely venturing out. Rather than simply writing such people off as idiots, can you instead look more deeply and discern vulnerability beneath their problematic behaviour? It won't always be easy, especially if their behaviours impinge unpleasantly on you, but in the long run compassionate understanding will always get you further and deeper than rejection and criticism.

QUESTIONS FOR REFLECTION

1. Now that you've read about the concept of self-compassion, what reactions do you notice within yourself? Does this feel like a helpful idea? Or do you notice, instead, a tendency to think that self-compassion will turn you into a softy?

2. In what ways do you tend to be critical of yourself? About your physical appearance? About your personality? About your intellectual abilities? Other areas of your life?

3. In what ways do you tend to be critical of other people?

4. How might compassion change your relationship with yourself, or with other people? Instead of saying 'no' (rejecting or demanding that things be different) to whatever aspect of life you find difficult, how might saying 'yes' change things for you? Is it possible to practise acceptance of yourself, of others, of life itself when it falls short of your hopes and demands?

5. Most people respond much better to praise than to criticism. If you want someone to do more of what you like, you need to praise them for the behaviours you like, rather than criticising the ones you don't. If this is true, how might you start to give yourself praise and encouragement? And other people?

6. How might the two wings of mindfulness and compassion make a difference for you?

FURTHER READING

Kate Joseph and Chris Irons (2018) *Managing Stress*. Pocket Study Skills Guides. London: Palgrave Macmillan.

This is a helpful guide for students, based on the principles of compassion-focused therapy.

Kristin Neff (2011) *Self-compassion: Stop Beating Yourself Up and Leave Insecurity Behind*. New York, NY: HarperCollins.

Kristin Neff has written a warm, encouraging book on how we can learn to be more compassionate towards ourselves and others. She also has a very good website with guided meditations and self-compassion practices: www.selfcompassion.org

REFERENCES

Barker, M.J. (2018) *Rewriting the Rules: An Anti Self-Help Guide to Love, Sex and Relationships*. London: Routledge.

Brach, T. (2003) *Radical Acceptance: Embracing Your Life with the Heart of a Buddha*. New York: Random House.

de Botton, A. (2005) *Status Anxiety*. London: Penguin.

Neff, K. (2011) *Self-compassion: Stop Beating Yourself Up and Leave Insecurity Behind*. New York, NY: HarperCollins.

Williams, M. and Penman, D. (2011) *Mindfulness: A Practical Guide to Finding Peace in a Frantic World*. London: Piatkus.

'IMAGINATION AND FICTION
MAKE UP MORE THAN
THREE QUARTERS OF
OUR REAL LIFE.,

Simone Weil,
*Gravity and
Grace* (1952)

5
MINDFULNESS
AND DEPRESSION

IN THIS CHAPTER YOU WILL:

- understand how unskilful thinking drives and sustains depression;

- learn about the typical thoughts that lie beneath depression;

- observe how mindfulness of thoughts can lessen the suffering that comes from inevitable pain in life;

- bring mindfulness to an everyday activity and appreciate how doing so can transform the most mundane of tasks;

- appreciate the role of self-compassion in helping you to respond well to your own sadness and fear.

Pete is in his second year at university. Well, actually, it's his third year because he dropped out of the second year after two terms because he felt so stressed and anxious about everything. Now he's back and starting second year again, but despite his hopes for a better experience this time, he can feel himself sliding back into the moods and behaviours that dragged him down the first time around. He sleeps until late morning, and then stays in bed until around 2pm. By that point, he's missed several lectures, most of his flatmates have been up and out for hours, and there's a sense of pointlessness in even trying to make anything of the day. Instead, he opens his laptop, spending hours watching YouTube videos, playing games, and he's recently started gambling too. Pete knows that he is getting into debt, though he tries not to think about it too much. While he was at home over the summer, Pete's girlfriend told him she didn't want to continue their relationship and that she was seeing someone else. Although he hasn't talked about it much, this has been pretty devastating for Pete. Sarah was his first serious relationship and Pete feels hurt and rejected, and he misses Sarah hugely. Pete actually feels desperate about how things are turning out for him; he knows his parents are very worried about him, but he avoids talking to them so that he doesn't have to answer their questions or feel their concern. He finds it really hard to talk about what is happening, and even to acknowledge his feelings to himself. He smokes a bit of weed at night to help him get to sleep, and to help him avoid the sense of despair that is gradually growing inside him. And then he wakes up and does it all again.

SADNESS IS A COMMON EMOTION

If anxiety is the most common problem that students talk about when they go for counselling at university, depression comes a close second. What *is* depression? It's a word that is bandied around fairly liberally and without much consistency. Is Pete depressed? Is there something physically wrong with him? Does he just need to 'pull himself together'? Should he take antidepressants? Or would getting into mindfulness help him at all?

'I'm feeling a bit depressed' is a sentence that can cover everything from the normal ups and downs of everyday life such as feeling blue or out of sorts, to a serious intent to self-harm, or even to take one's own life. It can be hard to know when a normal off day is turning into something more serious and when professional help might be needed. As already mentioned, mindfulness is not an alternative to professional help – whether from a GP, a therapist or even, in more acute situations, the A&E department of a hospital – but it can play a role in helping us to respond more compassionately to ourselves when we find ourselves being too self-critical or too pessimistic about the future.

RESPONDING TO PAIN WISELY

As with anxiety (see Chapter 7) how we respond to difficult emotions within ourselves is key and it is completely normal and appropriate to feel sad in many situations we will inevitably encounter in life, such as the end of a relationship we care about, being ill or someone we care about falling ill, or dying. Events in our immediate environment can have a huge impact on us too: things like noisy neighbours who play loud music at 3am every weekend, inconsiderate housemates who leave the kitchen in a filthy state despite being asked to clean up, racism, sexism, homo/bi/transphobia. Feeling sad, down, unhappy, scared, despairing are all completely normal responses to the way that life can unfold sometimes. These emotions tell us that we *care* about ourselves and our relationships. They tell us that we are human.

Nonetheless, despite the fact that many of these events are out of our control, how we respond to them may not be. There is a well-known saying in Buddhist thought: 'pain is inevitable; suffering is optional' (Ryan, 2017). This simply means that we cannot escape pain in life. We will get hurt and scarred as we make our way through a world where we do not control much of what feels important to us. But, perhaps, the depression and anxiety that can come to *dominate* our lives *is*, to some extent at least, optional.

The psychologist Martin Seligman believes that there are three fundamental beliefs that sustain depression, and which allow it get a foothold in our lives (Seligman, 2018):

1. This is all my fault.
2. I will always feel like this.
3. My whole life is ruined.

In other words, when we blame ourselves completely for whatever has happened (such as the end of a relationship), when we predict that this event will dominate the rest of our lives and when we tell ourselves that the feeling of sadness/loss will never change, depression is a predictable outcome. Seligman argues that certain people are more prone to such thinking patterns, and those of us who recognise this will acknowledge that we tend to ruminate (chew over) on these hopeless, depressing thoughts, and thus make our initial, normal reaction to pain much worse.

Clearly, then, mindfulness can help us to become more aware of suffering that is self-generated. There is another well-known story (Mindfulness Meditation, 2014), believed to originate with the Buddha himself, about how in life we cannot avoid being hit by painful arrows (the painful things that happen to all of us). However, with training, we can learn not to add to the pain of the first arrow by shooting another one into ourselves in the form of unskilful thinking.

Dr Albert Ellis, founder of rational emotive behaviour therapy (REBT), agreed that the way we *think and talk to ourselves* about difficult events can turn them into life-limiting tragedies. He devised a list of 'irrational' (that is, unhelpful because they defy reality) beliefs that are guaranteed to turn any drama into a crisis. You can search for REBT irrational beliefs on the internet and find Ellis's words very easily. Here are some of these beliefs:

1. I must succeed at everything I do. If I don't, I'm a complete and utter failure and I can't stand it.

2. The people I admire and respect in life must approve of me. If they don't, I am worthless.

3. I must be loved by the important people in my life. If they don't love me in the way I love them, I cannot stand it.

4. If things don't turn out the way I wanted them to, I can't stand it and I must feel depressed and anxious about this. I have no option but to spend a lot of time worrying and obsessing about what has happened.

5. If I feel upset or depressed, it's because of some external event that has happened. There's nothing I can do about how I feel; my feelings are out of my control.

6. When someone does something that hurts or upsets me, they are clearly bad people and I have no option other than to feel depressed about how they have treated me.

Ellis said that whenever we recognise depression in our lives we need to *cherchez le should* – in other words, identify where we are imposing a 'should' or 'must' onto a situation where it does not make sense. In essence, then, it is helpful to remember:

- Painful things will happen in life. This is inevitable.
- How you respond to those painful things can play a large part in determining how you feel about them.
- When you strongly believe that things *should/must* or *ought to be* different from how they are, you are fighting reality. Reality always wins.

HOW MINDFULNESS CAN HELP US AVOID THE 'SECOND ARROW'

We all tend to have repetitive, obsessive, unhelpful thoughts that our minds like to produce over and over again. Mindfulness teaches us that in order to avoid much suffering in life, we must become very familiar with those thoughts so that we don't keep getting swept away by them. On one mindfulness training I attended, the facilitator shared a useful metaphor for how mindfulness can help us, which I paraphrase here.

Imagine you are in a canoe, paddling along a beautiful river. It's a sunny day and the river is calm. Then, you notice that the water is starting to flow a bit faster and that your canoe is being pulled in a direction you don't want to go by some strong currents. You can hear the sound of rapids up ahead.

The river is your mind. The currents are thoughts that arise. Once you recognise thoughts that are unhelpful and that will lead you onto the rapids (get you into trouble, make you upset or unhelpfully sad), you can paddle to the shore, rest a while and decide how you want to continue your journey. Until you recognise those thoughts, you will find yourself continually swept over the rapids where the water (your mind) is upset and distressed. When this happens, self-compassion is essential: we all get swept over the rapids – even after months of mindfulness training. Learning to paddle to the shore takes much practice and self-compassion.

MINDFUL EXERCISE

When counselling students who are struggling with depression, I find that they are usually good at identifying the repetitive, unhelpful thoughts that keep sweeping them down the rapids. They already know, at some level, how they are talking to themselves. Take fifteen minutes now and allow yourself, without self-censoring, to write down the thoughts that are turning your own pain into suffering. Allow yourself to look into the suffering in your life, the distress, the depression, and simply acknowledge what you are telling yourself about whatever painful event triggered this suffering in you.

Thoughts about myself: 'I'm boring, I'm too fat; I must have deserved this to happen.'

Thoughts about other people: 'They don't feel like this, they are so much happier than me.'

Thoughts about the way the world is: 'It's all so unfair. No one cares about anyone but themselves.'

This is such an important exercise. Awareness precedes change. Until you are aware of the 'currents' in your mind, you will keep getting swept onto the rapids and into that churning state of depression. Once you become aware of these thoughts, you begin – slowly at first – to be able to decide whether to simply let those thoughts be, or whether to get some help in learning how to handle them. Some of the currents may be very powerful and you may find that it feels almost impossible not to keep getting swept away by them. That's when professional help can be invaluable.

OUR COLLECTIVE TENDENCY TOWARDS SELF-CRITICISM

When I have run mindfulness groups for students, one of the most powerful moments comes when I invite everyone to take a few sticky notes and, on each one, to write down the kind of unhelpful, self-bullying thoughts they recognise within their own minds. Usually, people are quite reluctant, at first, to acknowledge their own depressive thoughts, but after a few moments it can be hard to get people to stop. I then take these notes and, without disclosing who has written what, put them all up on a large board and then invite people to come and read what everyone else has written. We stand together and look at the thoughts on the board. Some of the examples include:

- 'I wish I was prettier.'
- 'I think I'm stupid.'
- 'I'm boring.'
- 'I'm too fat.'
- 'I want to be successful but I don't know how.'
- 'I'm no good at studying.'

This is always a powerful moment. As we stand together, reading the thoughts of other people, we all recognise: 'These are the thoughts I have about myself too.' After a few minutes, I invite people to share their experience of reading these thoughts.

- 'I never knew that everyone has the same thoughts as me.'
- 'It's sad that we all think like this.'
- 'It makes me feel better that other people think like I do too.'
- 'I wish we could stop thinking like this about ourselves.'

In fact, this is a profound moment of compassion. Sometimes there are even tears of sadness about the way we bully ourselves and put ourselves down. We recognise that we are prone to thinking badly about ourselves, and to comparing ourselves unfavourably with those around us. We also acknowledge that there is a very human tendency to be self-critical and negative about ourselves. That this is *not just me; it is everyone*. We recognise that we are all vulnerable human beings. With this exercise, people usually feel very clear that the other people in the group do not need to believe these thoughts about themselves, that they should be kinder to themselves. It is only one small logical further step to point out that if other people should be kinder to themselves, *so should you*.

RESPONDING TO INJUSTICE MINDFULLY

It's important to recognise that the 'solution' to depression need not only take the form of recognising and working with unhelpful thoughts. Depending on the situation, taking meaningful, mindful action is appropriate in an attempt to change unjust or oppressive actions or behaviours. Being mindful of the suffering caused by racism, for example, is not enough to alleviate suffering. Yet when we do decide that we must challenge policies, institutional practices or individual behaviours that are causing real pain in our own and others' lives, doing so mindfully (being aware of our own motivations, of the limits of our ability to control certain situations) is important for our own sanity. If we only *react*, rather than *respond*, we are likely to make things worse for ourselves because of the suffering we create within ourselves. Taking mindful action is a delicate skill to learn. Perhaps we can find wisdom in a secular version of the Serenity Prayer as we contemplate what action is appropriate:

Grant me the serenity to accept the things I cannot change

Courage to change the things I can and must change

And the wisdom to know the difference. (Baggini, 2016)

Sadness of all kinds, from mild to intense, can be an appropriate response to difficult life circumstances. Our sadness should never be minimised, dismissed or avoided. Grief is a powerful emotion that needs special attention and that is often misunderstood or dismissed in our culture. It is important that our natural human response to loss, to disappointment, to pain, is allowed expression. Yet, as we are coming to see, our natural human emotions can very easily descend into depression, which takes hold of our lives and turns the original pain into ongoing emotional suffering. Depression thrives in an atmosphere of self-blame, self-pity and self-doubt. Mindfulness, with its opportunity to observe *without* self-blame, self-pity or self-doubt those unhelpful thoughts, offers us an escape route from the downward spiral of suffering; it can help us to discern when taking action to try to deal with outward sources of pain is appropriate; and it can help us to perceive when, despite the pain we are experiencing being intense, we will only make things worse by fighting against the reality of life.

Depression can be a complex experience, and many of us may need help in unravelling the various threads that have become tangled and are tripping us up. Usually, the causes of depression are not biological and antidepressants will never help with dealing with unrealistic or unhelpful thought patterns (Breeding, 2016) – even though they may provide some relief and enable us to be able to start doing the work we need to do in order to free ourselves from our suffering. This takes courage, persistence and self-compassion. Mindfulness offers gentle ways to deliberately and consciously focus our attention away from unhelpful thinking and to engage with the often-forgotten daily miracles that make up our daily lives.

MINDFUL EXERCISE

In Japan, the tea ceremony is a rich example of mindfulness in practice. The ceremony is full of ritual and symbolism. What could otherwise be a mindless procedure is given great attention and dignity, and is thus transformed. While you may not feel up to performing a full Japanese tea ceremony (though if you get the chance, do try to observe one), you can transform the making of a cup of tea in your own kitchen through mindful attention.

Prepare yourself internally for this exercise: take a few slow, deep breaths and recognise that you are going to perform your own version of a tea ceremony; that you are going to bring full attention to every aspect of what is usually a rushed, barely noticed routine.

Now choose a cup or mug, one that you like. You can buy yourself a beautiful mug if you like, especially for this practice. Put clean, fresh water into a kettle. As you do so, be mindful that the water flowing from your tap is a kind of miracle: clean, fresh, freely available – brought to you through the hard work of countless individuals.

● ● ● ●

Then switch on your kettle. Again, be aware of the luxury of having electricity freely available, the result of much hard work by countless individuals you will never know.

As you wait for the kettle to boil, try to stay focused on sounds: the gentle creaks and groans from the kettle; the way the sound changes as the heat increases; the sound of water bubbling and boiling; steam emerging from the spout; the 'click' as the kettle switches itself off.

Then pour the water into your mug, over your chosen tea. Be aware of any aromas rising from your mug as you stir the tea. Then wait for four to five minutes to let the tea fully infuse into the water. As you wait, bring your awareness to the tea itself: Where was it grown? Who grew it? Who picked it? Packed it? Transported it? Here in your mug is a miracle of interdependence: the sun, the rain, the earth – all here in your mug, along with traces of each individual who has brought it safely to you.

When the time is up, mindfully add milk, lemon or sugar to your tea, if you like, and then slowly raise the mug to your mouth and take the first sip.

Savour the taste, heat and aroma of this miraculous mug of tea.

Feel yourself swallow the liquid.

Then sit quietly somewhere and drink the rest of your tea. When your mind wanders, or you feel an itch to 'do something', gently take some deep breaths and bring your focus back to your tea. The feel of the mug in your hand, the sight and aroma of the tea, the way the temperature of the tea gradually changes as time passes.

When you finish, wash your mug carefully, dry it and put it away, ready for the next time.

This exercise is a gentle way of engaging with mindfulness when you are not feeling up to formal sitting meditation. You can combine this with an eating meditation or mindful walking.

It's worth reiterating that mindfulness is not meant to be the solution to all our problems in the way we have come to think about this in the West. 'Give me a pill/a technique that will fix me.' Mindfulness is a way of being, and is part of a wider ethical and philosophical pathway that will, if practised wholeheartedly, liberate us from the tyranny of harmful thoughts. This does not happen overnight. We are slowly building awareness – the container for our habitual reactions, thoughts and behaviours – and cultivating compassion, freeing ourselves from the self-bullying and criticism that only adds to our pain. We come to see that the pain we each feel is the pain felt throughout the world by countless people; *my* pain is *your* pain; *your* pain is *my* pain. Suffering, while perhaps difficult to eradicate completely, can be curtailed and softened by my own reactions and skill in handling it.

When Pete began to practise some simple mindfulness exercises – and particularly when he learned the key importance of self-compassion – he began to see more clearly that the way he was talking to himself about the things that were happening in his life were just making them worse. He was blaming himself completely for Sarah leaving him and he was being very self-critical about his failure of the second year on his course. All of this was merely undermining his ability to respond in a gentler way to the undoubtedly harsh knocks he had suffered. It was really hard for Pete to accept that his harsh thinking – the 'second arrow' – was not 'the truth', but rather an unnecessarily bullying voice based on his deep fear of letting anyone see his vulnerabilities. Pete spent some time in therapy, learning to talk about his fears and insecurities: slowly, he is starting to learn to 'paddle the canoe' to the banks of the river rather than perpetually being swept over into the rapids of self-loathing and self-condemnation.

QUESTIONS FOR REFLECTION

1. Do you recognise that sometimes you shoot a second arrow into yourself after something difficult has happened to you? How do you tend to do this? Self-criticism? Self-pitying? Complaining about how unfair life is?

2. When you are facing difficult situations in life, as we all have to, how might self-compassion help you to respond more helpfully on those occasions?

3. Do you think that you might need to reach out for professional help to help you cope with a particularly difficult event that you have faced?

4. Are you measuring yourself, your life, against unhelpful and unrealistic standards that you wouldn't apply to anyone else? Can you recognise this and mindfully step back from doing this?

FURTHER READING

Russ Harris (2012) *The Reality Slap: How to Find Fulfilment When Life Hurts*. London: Constable & Robinson.

A warm and wise voice, helping us to face the inevitable pain that comes our way as part of life. The author incorporates mindful practice with psychological insights.

Mark Williams and John Teasdale (2007) *The Mindful Way through Depression: Freeing Yourself from Chronic Unhappiness*. New York: Guilford Press.

Extensive practices, and guided meditations, to cultivate mindful awareness of thoughts and an ability to 'let them go', rather than trying to think our way out of sadness.

REFERENCES

Baggini, J. (2016) Presentation at Heads of University Counselling Services meeting, Manchester Metropolitan University.

Breeding, J. (2016) College counselling in the age of biological psychiatry. *University and College Counselling*, May 4(2): 4-9.

Mindfulness Meditation (2014) The second arrow. Available at: http://mindfulnessmeditation.net.au/arrow/ (accessed 20 January 2019).

Ryan, E. (2017) Pain is inevitable, suffering is optional. Available at: https://mytherapist.ie/pain-inevitable-suffering-optional/ (accessed 20 January 2019).

Seligman, M. (2018) *Learned Optimism: How to Change Your Mind and Your Life*. London: Nicholas Brealey Publishing.

Weil, S. (1952) *Gravity and Grace*. London: Routledge & Kegan Paul.

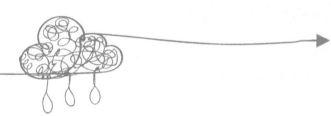

'THERE IS NO WAY TO
GENUINELY, POWERFULLY,
TRULY
LOVE
YOURSELF
WHILE CRAFTING A MASK OF
PERFECTION. '

Vironika Tugaleva (2016)

6
MINDFULNESS
AND
PERFECTIONISM

IN THIS CHAPTER YOU WILL:

- explore the phenomenon of perfectionism and understand how it is an unhelpful driver for your studies;

- begin to identify the kinds of thoughts and beliefs that can lead you to view academic results as an indicator of your entire worth as a person;

- begin to understand that making mistakes, failing, acknowledging errors is fundamental to human growth and development, and how perfectionism inhibits this essential aspect of life.

Maya is a medic, studying hard and feeling under intense pressure to keep up with her course mates who all seem to be getting through the huge amount of work much more easily than she is. And they have time for a social life. When she compares herself to others, Maya feels intense anxiety: she has a strong belief that she must do better than them if she is to maintain any credibility. Deep down, she still can't really believe that she is at university, studying medicine. 'Surely', she thinks, 'proper doctors never have the anxiety, the self-doubt and the insecurity that plague me?' Maya is desperate to hide her sense of inadequacy from everyone: friends, tutors, welfare staff. She finds herself studying each day until past midnight, frantically trying to get through everything she feels she needs to do, but she never has a sense that she has done enough. Weekends are spent in the library, reading, making notes, practising multiple-choice questions. She feels completely exhausted; she's not eating well and she's losing touch with friends and family because she feels she mustn't spend long socialising when she should be working. Next year, placements start and she's extremely anxious about coping with consultants and other professionals in front of her peer group: she fears that the extent of her ignorance will be revealed and that she's likely to be kicked off her course. Maya feels trapped: her family are so proud that she is studying to become a doctor, so she never tells them how unhappy and stressed she feels, but she's starting to wonder if she will actually make it through the course at all.

PERFECTIONISM

This can be defined as that intense feeling that only the very best will do, that there is always one more reference or paper to check before you start to write that essay; the sense that you are in competition with everyone on your course and must come out on top, rather than simply trying to do your best. It is the sense that so many of us have that no matter how much we do, it's never enough, and that we will have to work every moment of every day if we are to achieve our full potential. It's the belief that nothing less than one hundred per cent is acceptable in terms of academic results, that only a first will do when it comes to an undergraduate degree and only a distinction at Master's. It is a problem that affects thousands of students: arriving at university, far from reassuring them that they deserve their place on their course and that they have the intellectual capacity to cope with their studies, sets off the opposite belief : 'Everyone else belongs here except me'.

Closely allied to perfectionism is a state of mind known as impostor syndrome – the belief that 'I am a fraud' and 'I only got into university by some fluke or mistake on the part of whoever made the decision that I could come'.

Perfectionism + impostor syndrome = a completely miserable life

When you are in the grip of perfectionism, your thinking becomes rigid, full of 'shoulds' and 'musts' ('I must work all the time', 'I should be able to write an essay perfectly first time round', 'I need to be doing better than everyone else in order to feel OK about myself'). This kind of thinking is allied with a deep-seated sense that nothing you ever do is enough. Stress builds, there are huge amounts of guilt; depression is never far away and a healthy work–life balance is completely neglected. As with Maya, social life, exercise, fun can seem like a distraction from the 'real' business of being a student: studying.

Here are some typical thoughts and beliefs that might suggest you're experiencing the stressful results of perfectionism and/or impostor syndrome:

- 'I *must* get a first.'
- 'Everyone finds the work easier than me.'
- 'If I don't understand something, it means I'm stupid.'
- 'I can't cope with the idea of asking a question in a seminar in case it makes me look stupid.'
- 'If a tutor asks me a question in a seminar, I must be able to give really clear and intelligent answers.'
- 'I shouldn't have to ask for any help in doing my work.'

- 'I'm only here because they felt sorry for me or made a mistake when they were letting me in.'
- 'I should be working' (*all* the time).

All of these thoughts are extremely anxiety-provoking and will leave you feeling hopeless and useless. Yet you may, until now, have felt that those thoughts and feelings actually reflect the truth. That's one of the problems with perfectionism. You think, 'Well, yes, it's obviously true that I have to push myself really hard. If I don't, I won't work and that would be a disaster.' Or, 'I work best under pressure. So, if I'm not hard on myself, or tell myself that I must get a first, then I'll just give up and waste my time doing nothing.' It can seem to be simple logic that aiming for perfection is the ideal to which we should all aspire. After all, surely no one wants to settle for anything less than perfection, do they?

This rigid, all-or-nothing thinking comes from the false belief that it's possible to be perfect and avoid all mistakes in life. It's a kind of magical thinking based on the sense that if only you work incredibly hard, you'll be able to control the outcome of your degree and make sure that you get the job and the career that you want. One of the important things we all have to learn as we go through life is that important outcomes are never guaranteed. There is no law of the universe that states that 'If I do x hours of work, I am guaranteed a first'. There is, equally, no law of the universe that makes it inevitable that you will get the job you want simply because you happen to achieve that first. Equally, no matter how hard we try, as human beings we will always slip up, make mistakes, fall short: that's just how it is. For Maya, of course, as with other professionals who are training to care for other people such as pilots, lawyers, financial advisers, the stakes can seem frighteningly high. The price of imperfection, of making a mistake, can cause huge suffering and have serious implications. Yet, that is life. No matter how hard we try, any of us can, at any time, make a mistake that has serious consequences, even though we had only the best of intentions.

Perfectionism is based on fear; fear that you're not good enough; that you have to prove yourself constantly and that nothing less than the absolute best is acceptable; that if you don't achieve the highest results, your life will be a disaster. This is often, too, based on a mistaken belief that the only way you can make yourself lovable is by always achieving excellent academic results. Presentations, degrees, exams all come to mean much more than they are intended to: they become the way you try to prove to yourself and others that you're OK and that you are, in fact, lovable. Inevitably, you never actually succeed in feeling lovable, because presentations, exams and degrees aren't able to confer that sense on any of us: there may be a momentary sense of satisfaction when a great result is achieved, but then it's on to the next challenge with barely a pause. Your self-esteem becomes dependent on outcomes, which leaves you in a very precarious position of always feeling that you need to get outstanding results. Because academic success – or any success based on performance – is unable to provide us with lasting satisfaction and self-esteem, you have to address those needs in other, more meaningful ways, primarily through relationships where you can come to know that you are accepted and loved just as you are, warts and all.

HOW MIGHT MINDFULNESS HELP WITH PERFECTIONISM AND IMPOSTOR SYNDROME?

As you're learning, mindfulness is not about stopping thoughts, getting rid of them or sitting in judgement on them. So often we say to ourselves: 'I must stop thinking like this!' or 'I'm such a fool. I know it's stupid to do all this work, but I simply can't stop myself.'

Change is not possible without awareness. Until you recognise the kind of thoughts you are having, they control you. So, to some extent, mindfulness here is about simply recognising the typical, repetitive thoughts that your mind likes to create for you, and the deeper beliefs that drive those thoughts, when what you have decided to do is sit and be still. As you know, thoughts will distract you – not occasionally, but constantly. However, as you practise, you will, slowly but surely, become more and more familiar with the kind of perfectionistic thoughts (the perfectionistic monkey) that are likely to distract you. They could be something like this:

- 'This is a waste of time! I should be working!'
- 'I'm not doing this right. I'm sure other people are much better at practising mindfulness than me! I must try harder!'
- 'I'm a complete phoney. I'm supposed to be sitting and focusing on my breath, but all I can do is think about getting back to work.'
- 'How is this supposed to be helping me? I just feel frustrated. I'm going to stop and get on with some work.'
- 'I'm probably going to be a fantastic meditator. I wonder if I should start teaching others how to do this?'

These thoughts are not your fault. Your mind has simply got used to producing them for you. It can be really hard to continue to sit and practise mindfulness when your mind is busy producing these thoughts for you. But, as we saw, you can train yourself (and patience is required) to *notice the thoughts and let them be*. You don't *have to* react to the thoughts and you don't *need to* criticise yourself for having them; you *can* just let them go. This is not just *part* of the process; it *is* the process, becoming more and more familiar with your thinking mind, and simply allowing yourself to observe what is happening.

MINDFUL EXERCISE

Find somewhere to sit that is quiet and where you won't be disturbed. Give yourself a nice stretch of time for this exercise. Try not to do it when you're feeling stressed or when you have an important meeting coming up ahead. Take slow, deep breaths. Imagine your lungs are like a sponge – each time you breathe out, you are squeezing the sponge so that it is empty of air, and as you inhale, the sponge fills again with air. Put more effort into the 'squeeze' – breathe out really deeply, making sure that you exhale all the way, and then allow your lungs to naturally fill again with as much air as they need. Do this a few times. When you feel ready, gently close your eyes, or lower your gaze.

Then let your breathing return to normal – just let it steady back down to a natural, unrushed rhythm.

Let your attention settle on your breath. Keep it there, gently following each in-breath and each out-breath. Do this for several minutes. Place a hand over your heart and hold it there gently.

When your attention wanders, just make a mental note of where it has wandered to. Every time your thoughts are self-critical, self-judging, put a hand over your heart and gently say to yourself: 'It's OK. It's just a thought.' Or: 'Let it go. It's just a thought.' Your hand over your heart is a sign to yourself that you are showing compassion and caring to yourself, and that you are allied with a loving intent rather than a critical one. Keep your hand gently in place while you continue to focus on your breathing for several more moments. Each time a critical, worrying thought creeps back in, gently press your hand against your chest and repeat a soothing response.

After you have sat quietly for the time that you have set aside, take one final deep breath and, as you exhale, let your hand return to its natural position, gently open your eyes or lift your gaze, and sit quietly for a minute.

What came up for you in this exercise? What kind of distracting thoughts? Some of them are likely to have been overly self-critical or self-judging. Just notice this now; notice any tendency to be hard on yourself and to pull yourself down, and in particular, any anxiety-provoking thoughts that are giving you unhelpful, unrealistic messages about how you approach your work.

LISTEN TO THE AUDIO CLIP AT
https://study.sagepub.com/mindfulness

FRAMING YOUR THOUGHTS

Mindfulness can help us to recognise our typical, unhelpful repetitive thoughts and, rather than simply getting carried away by them, to put a frame around them, sit back and observe them. 'Putting a frame' around thoughts can be a helpful process to hold in mind; you might even find it helpful to write down your typical perfectionistic beliefs and impostor syndrome thoughts – maybe those that came up in the mindfulness exercise above – and draw a picture frame around them. That way, when they come back (and they will) you are already prepared and able, with practice, to recognise them for what they are: 'mental events' (Williams and Penman, 2011) rather than 'the truth'.

Mindfulness is not about getting rid of thoughts. It is about observing them and recognising that they are not necessarily 'the truth'. We have become conditioned to produce certain kinds of thoughts (by our culture, our family upbringing, our schooling) but that doesn't necessarily make them helpful to us. With gentle, compassionate, mindful attention, we can become much more aware of the kinds of conditioning that have created insecurity or competitiveness within us, and gradually, as we build the container for our thoughts (see Chapter 1), become less driven by that conditioning.

MINDFUL EXERCISE

In this exercise, you're going to spend some time standing back from your life, exploring where some of the beliefs you have about yourself and about what is necessary to achieve love have come from. It might be helpful to do this exercise with a trusted friend, or a therapist who will help you to think about some of these questions.

Take some time to get comfortable: remind yourself that this exercise is not a test. You may like to have some photos of yourself as a young child to look at to help you get in touch with some of the feelings and thoughts you have picked up from family, friends, your social environment.

Try not to censor your responses to these questions – just write freely whatever comes into your head.

- In your family, what kind of behaviour earned praise? Being kind? Working hard? Being funny? Self-sacrifice? Something else?

- In your family, what kind of behaviour attracted criticism or punishment? Being emotional? Being silly? Something else?

- Whatever your gender, how do you think your family responded to this aspect of you? Were you treated differently because of your gender? Were there different expectations because of your gender?

- Do you have siblings? If so, how did you feel in comparison with them as you grew up? Equal? Inferior? Superior? Something else? If you had no siblings, how might this have impacted on the sense of expectation that your parents had of you?

- Who did/do you most admire in your family, extended family, or your circle of friends? What is it that you admire about them?

- What was your experience of school like? Was it fun? Were you bullied? Did work ever become an escape from painful circumstances?

- What kind of comments did your performance at school attract from family? Praise and encouragement, no matter what the results? A sense that you could have done better, no matter what the results? Disappointment? Criticism? Pride?

- Within the context you grew up in, and comparing yourself to others around your own age (siblings, cousins, friends), how do you think you were seen by others? Clever? Slow? Very intelligent? Needing to work hard to achieve anything good? Were there any nicknames for you that you remember? 'The quiet one', 'the brainy one', 'the sporty one'?

These questions are designed to help you reflect on the kinds of influences you have had growing up and that will have helped to shape your sense of self, and your sense of how important academic work was (or not) to your self-worth and to your lovability. As you think about your responses, what is your overriding feeling? Sadness? Appreciation? Blankness? Anger? Something else?

These questions are not intended to lead you to blame anyone else, or yourself, for the way things are now. They are simply there to help raise your awareness of the kinds of conditioning that have impacted on how you view academic work and their significance in determining your worth as a person.

For Maya, it was a real struggle to make time to sit in formal mindfulness meditation. She had to contend with a powerful urge to continually put off her periods of practice. After joining a campus mindfulness group and gaining some insight into how her mind was actually producing unhelpful thoughts for her, and why (a high premium on academic achievement in her culture, the impact of having a very successful older brother who she was constantly trying to match up to), Maya was able to create some space between her thoughts and her behaviour. Although it was uncomfortable at times, committing to practice mindfulness in a group began to give Maya a different perspective on what was important and a sense that she wanted to create more balance and acceptance in her life.

QUESTIONS FOR REFLECTION

1. What are your typical, repetitive perfectionistic and impostor syndrome thoughts and beliefs? Take five minutes now and write down as many as you can. Then put that list somewhere you will be able to remind yourself, from time to time, of the thoughts your mind produces about your academic abilities. Once you have your list of typical thoughts, take some time to remind yourself that *thoughts are not necessarily the truth*.

2. Imagine you are going for an interview. You are asked the question: 'Tell us about a mistake you've made that had serious consequences and how you coped with that.' Consider what your own attitude is towards making mistakes. Do you try very hard to avoid them? Do you try to hide them when you make them? Or do you see mistakes as opportunities to learn?

3. When the Navajo Indians weave a carpet, they deliberately include a 'mistake' as a way of reminding themselves that only God is perfect (Anderson, 2012). In what way might you make a deliberate mistake today? Include a typo in an essay? Arrive slightly late for a lecture? Something else? What is your emotional reaction to this suggestion? 'Ridiculous. What's the point?' Sometimes, however, perfectionism can be confronted by deliberately including an error in our work – and learning from the outcome that our fears of what will happen if we slip up are usually greatly exaggerated.

FURTHER READING

Brené Brown (2010) *The Gifts of Imperfection: Let Go of Who You Think You're Supposed to Be and Embrace Who You Are.* Center City, MN: Hazelden.

This author is passionate about the need for all of us to compassionately and bravely acknowledge our vulnerability and writes compellingly about why this is essential for deep and authentic relationships.

Yong Kang Chan (2017) *Empty Your Cup: Why We Have Low Self-esteem and How Mindfulness Can Help.* Yong Kang Chan.

A simply written book by an author who is searingly honest about his own struggle with low self-esteem. He presents a vivid model of how mindfulness has the potential to transform the self-critical voice in our minds.

REFERENCES

Anderson, D. (2012) Deliberate mistakes. Available at: http://findingyoursoul.com/2012/06/deliberate-mistakes/ (accessed 23 January 2019).

Tugaleva, V. (2016) 16 October. Available at: https://www.facebook.com/vironika.tugalev/posts/1091068217681048 (accessed 15 August 2019).

Williams, M. and Penman, D. (2011) *Mindfulness: A Practical Guide to Finding Peace in a Frantic World.* London: Piatkus.

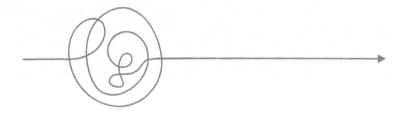

"**ANXIETY** WAS BORN IN THE VERY SAME MOMENT AS MANKIND. AND SINCE WE WILL NEVER BE ABLE TO MASTER IT, WE WILL HAVE TO LEARN TO LIVE WITH IT—

JUST AS WE HAVE LEARNED TO LIVE WITH STORMS."

Paulo Coelho, *Manuscript Found in Accra* (2013)

7
MINDFULNESS
AND
ANXIETY

IN THIS CHAPTER YOU WILL:

- explore why anxiety is such a common problem among students;

- gain understanding of what drives anxiety so that you can be more self-compassionate towards your own experience of anxiety;

- consider how mindfulness may offer some relief from anxiety-provoking thoughts and bodily reactions;

- see how many of our usual ways to avoid anxiety unintentionally make it stronger.

Gabriela is an international student who has come to the UK to study for a PhD. Before she arrived, she felt excited – looking forward to a big adventure, to meeting new friends and colleagues, and to working with a supervisor who was renowned in her field of work. Gabriela has been at university for about four months, and the feelings of excitement have given way to a kind of dread – a feeling that she has made a huge mistake in travelling so far to live and study alone. Instead of feeling excited, she feels constant anxiety about her new situation. A tension in her stomach means that she is eating very little; she feels quite nauseous and tense a lot of the time. She has met her supervisor once, briefly, and since then feels that she has been left to her own devices, to figure out what she is supposed to do. Other researchers have been working together for some time, and she doesn't feel that they are welcoming or interested in her. She gets up each morning, goes into her office, and then goes home again with very little social contact. The weather is cold and wet; the evenings are dark. She has real problems understanding the local accent and hasn't made any British friends so far. She feels lonely and unsupported – missing her family and friends from home and wondering how she will get through the next three to four years of her life if they are going to be like this. At night, sleep is difficult; she can feel her heart beating loudly as she lies in bed; she cries often. In her mind, the thoughts go round and round: 'What's wrong with me? Why can't I make this work? Why am I being so stupid?'

Anxiety among students is extremely common. More and more students are presenting for counselling and requesting 'reasonable adjustments' and 'special conditions' for coursework and exams. There is much speculation about the causes of this anxiety, including suggestions that young people are less resilient nowadays compared with previous generations – that they have been 'coddled' by over-protective, well-intentioned parents, and that they cannot cope when they have to face the realities of life alone. Ideas that the internet and social media have created an environment where expectations of how individuals 'should' be have escalated beyond what is attainable or reasonable for individuals to achieve: perfect bodies, fantastic careers, enormous wealth and fame. Additionally, real-world pressures, such as tuition fees, student debt and career prospects, undoubtedly add to the fundamental demands of courses intentionally designed to stretch you and take you to the limits of your abilities and knowledge. In addition, there can often be a sense that feeling anxious is wrong, something to get rid of and be free from.

Yet, anxiety, far from being a strange or unusual emotion, is a fundamental part of our biological make-up. Cast your mind back to the reptilian brain we encountered in Chapter 2 – that part of the brain that is concerned only with survival. This powerful, often unconscious, part of our brains constantly scans our environment for potential threats to our safety. Human beings have evolved to be the most successful and dominant species on our planet in part because of our ability to predict danger, to imagine 'what might go wrong' and take preventative actions. We are expert at seeing risks and devising solutions to overcome those dangers.

However, the reptilian brain is not good at distinguishing between real and imagined threat, and it can also be stimulated by small changes in the environment. If you move to a new house or a new town (as when you move away from home to start at university), your 'threat system' – your automatic self-protection mechanism – is switched 'on' and stays on until you have established new routines and habits that allow it to stand down – for the time being. Some people have a more sensitive threat system than others; for these people, their threat system will get activated more often, more strongly and for longer than for others. So, for instance, arriving at university for the first time, your threat system will be on high alert as your brain sifts and sorts through all the new inputs it is receiving: new sights, new sounds, new people, new demands. This is a lot to take in and it may take much longer than you anticipate until your wonderfully protective threat system goes into stand-by mode. Your reptilian brain is simply trying to establish how safe your new environment is – something that takes time.

In addition to our interaction with our physical environments, we now also have to cope with virtual reality. Many of us spend hours a day interacting via social media and while we are not entirely clear about the impact this has on our threat system, it does appear to have a significant effect on how we evaluate ourselves. Communicating with people we may never meet, and the viewing of thousands of images online is not something our brains have evolved to handle. A hundred years ago, if you lived in a small village, you might encounter a hundred or so people in your life; now, in our virtual worlds, you 'meet' thousands. Their life stories, their images and their achievements all impact on you and on your primitive survival systems.

As mentioned above, our reptilian brains are not good at distinguishing between real and imagined threats. When you put your hand down on a hot surface, you react and pull your hand away before you've even fully registered or understood what is happening. That's your physical threat system working to protect you from an immediate, physical threat. But your emotional threat system gets switched 'on' if your higher brain starts to produce thoughts such as 'I must get a first' or 'I'll make a terrible fool of myself if I ask a question in a seminar'. Exams, presentations, interviews, even walking into a lecture theatre, can all trigger your threat system with its fight, flight or freeze response, even though none of those situations are actually life-threatening.

CAN YOU GET RID OF ANXIETY?

'I just want to stop feeling anxious all the time' was a very common plea from students I met in the university counselling service where I worked for many years. There was an understandable desire to be free from anxiety, to be calm and confident all the time, and to never feel the twinges of uncertainty and fear that seem to bedevil so many students' lives. And while many students' anxiety is the result of their threat system being stimulated by new environments, social media and unhelpful repetitive thoughts, there are other students who experience a different kind of anxiety: an existential anxiety that relates to the meaning of life and the difficulty in finding a sense of meaning for existence. The phrase *existential angst* captures this kind of anxiety which, again, is common to nearly everyone when we stop and consider the meaning of life. What am I here for? Is there a purpose to life beyond my own small ambitions? What happens when I die? This kind of anxiety can tip over into depression (see Chapter 5) as you start to grapple with the larger-life questions that have kept philosophers, theologians, psychologists and others occupied for millennia.

Although anxiety in and of itself can be uncomfortable to experience, a bigger problem with anxiety is our reaction to it. Hopefully, you can now see that the experience of anxiety is a basic part of being human: we all have different sensitivities to new situations that we face, and we all have different responses to the existential questions that arise from our human condition. But anxiety – fear – is normal, natural and not something we ever could or should get rid of. The quest to 'stop feeling anxious' is, in fact, a quest to stop being human.

Even so, we often beat ourselves up for feeling anxious. As we saw with Gabriela, who is facing enormous challenges and whose threat system is switched to 'full on', thoughts such as 'What's wrong with me?', 'I'm such an idiot for feeling like this' or 'I'm such a loser, no one else feels this way' actually increase our suffering. We condemn ourselves for our only-too-human responses to the challenges of life. It is really important to be clear with yourself: anxiety is normal and not something to 'get rid of'.

WORKING *WITH* ANXIETY AND NOT *AGAINST* IT

What you *may* need to work with, gently and with self-compassion, is your own reaction to your anxiety, to the self-bullying that occurs as you condemn yourself for your ordinary human vulnerability. None of us is superman or superwoman. All of us (yes, everyone) is vulnerable. Whether that is in the face of challenges in the here-and-now (noisy flatmates, a big presentation, a difficult relationship) or challenges on a broader canvas (what do I want my life to be about?), what we need is to develop a new, compassionate relationship with our anxiety. To be human is to experience anxiety.

Sometimes people are told when they discuss their concerns that they have 'generalised anxiety disorder' or are given some other diagnosis that implies that anxiety is a problem that can be cured, that it is an illness. Of course, sometimes anxiety can take over a person's life to such an extent that they do need specialist interventions – for example, with obsessive compulsive disorder (OCD) where anxiety has given rise to 'magic' rituals that must be performed in an attempt (usually futile) to ward off imagined danger, or with phobias that are interfering with the quality of a person's life. But the fundamental experience of anxiety is not the problem; it is our reaction to our anxiety which so often becomes a problem – we try to get rid of anxiety, we pretend that we never experience it and we criticise ourselves mercilessly for feeling unsure of ourselves in new situations.

I invite you now to stop for a moment and think about your own experience of anxiety. These questions may help you to explore it, and you may find it helpful to write about your responses or talk about them with someone you trust:

- Do you think you are more or less anxious than most people around you?
- What situations tend to make you most anxious? Social situations? Work? Being alone? Other?
- How do you respond to your anxiety? Do you get anxious about being anxious? Do you get depressed about being anxious? Do you try to escape from anxiety by avoiding any situation where your threat system gets switched on? Are you self-compassionate towards your anxiety?
- What coping strategies do you have towards your anxiety?

What do you do to try to *not* feel anxious? Drink? Drugs? Eat? Exercise? Self-harm? Sleep?

- How does anxiety affect your quality of life? Do you avoid things you'd like to do because of your anxiety? Or are you able to accept that feeling anxious is unavoidable in new situations and not allow it to stop you from doing what is important to you?

You may feel that, after answering those questions, anxiety is playing a large part in preventing you from living as fully and freely as you could. If so, just be mindful of any immediate reaction to criticise yourself or put yourself down: this will not help you. Your task is to learn to take care of your anxiety, to allow it and to reassure it, almost as though that part of you is a small child needing the reassurance of a loving, caring parent.

HOW CAN MINDFULNESS HELP ME WITH ANXIETY?

As we have already seen, mindfulness is, in part, about becoming familiar with the workings of our minds – allowing our unruly monkey minds to 'just be' – learning to see our thoughts as *just* thoughts rather than commands to be obeyed, and deliberately and consciously coming into the present moment where, usually, things are survivable. Mindfulness, then, offers a vantage point from which we can adopt an observer position towards our unruly minds without immediately reacting to the thoughts they produce for us. This ability takes practice (*simple, not easy*) and you may need support in doing this, particularly if your reaction to your anxiety has become a significant feature of your life such as in OCD. Remember that mindfulness is not a substitute for professional help – you cannot do a spiritual bypass on major trauma or difficulties – but, with appropriate guidance, it can be a transformational way of stepping out of the incessant, unhelpful chatter of monkey mind and developing a more compassionate perspective on the vulnerabilities of our human condition.

MINDFUL EXERCISE

Find somewhere to sit that is relatively peaceful and where you won't be disturbed. Decide how long you want to sit for – five or ten minutes is good. Take some deep, slow breaths – make the out-breath slightly longer than the in-breath.

Remind yourself of your intention for taking this time now: to move beyond your thinking mind into a space where you simply and compassionately observe everything that arises in these moments – thoughts, feelings, bodily sensations – without feeling that you have to change anything.

Close your eyes when you feel ready or lower your gaze. Tune in to the feeling of sitting: feel your weight on your chair or cushion, the pressure in your feet on the floor, your hands resting on your legs, the feeling of your breath. Bring your attention to your breathing, just following the flow of air in and out of your body, not forcing or changing it, just observing. Make your breath the focus of your attention now for as long as you have decided to sit.

Whenever your attention wanders away from your breath, simply make a mental note of what draws your mind away: give each thought or sensation a simple label such as thinking, worrying, planning, remembering and then return to your breath. Depending on how you are in this moment, your mind may wander very frequently. Try not to judge yourself; just label your thought and come back to the breath.

When your time for sitting is up, bring your attention back to your body. Open your eyes and take a moment to register the kind of thoughts your mind was producing for you as you sat. Anxiety-based thoughts? Worries about the future or regrets about the past?

Take a moment to congratulate yourself for sitting with those thoughts and allowing them to just be without reacting to them. If you found it hard to let the thoughts just be and you became embroiled in them for longer than you intended, gently remind yourself that it takes time to develop the observing position in mindfulness that will enable you to *respond* appropriately rather than *react* instinctively to your thoughts.

LISTEN TO THE AUDIO CLIP AT
https://study.sagepub.com/mindfulness

Mindfulness is not a relaxation technique. It is not about banishing anxiety. However, it *is* about helping you to become familiar with the kind of repetitive, worrying thoughts that your mind produces for you and helping you see those thoughts as *just* thoughts. And, perhaps with support from others, to assess whether the thoughts are helpful for you (can you take meaningful action to lessen the fears?) or unhelpful (such as worrying about or trying too hard to control the outcomes of exams/presentations). Mindfulness can help you to recognise thoughts as unhelpful, to gradually become more able to let those thoughts be, and to allow them to run their course without your interference or trying to stop them or change them.

MINDFULNESS WHEN ANXIETY IS HIGH

Sometimes, sitting meditation may simply feel too difficult if your mind is highly active and anxiety has gone beyond a certain level. You may feel agitated and distressed. In such circumstances, you may need to gently allow yourself to practise mindfulness in a different way.

Walking meditation (see Chapter 3) is a good way to be mindful when monkey mind is in full swing. Focusing on the movement of your whole body rather than the breath may help to calm you down, or to distract yourself from intrusive thoughts, if you can allow yourself to simply focus on walking, movement and breath.

You can also try the following mindful exercise:

MINDFUL EXERCISE

Sit on a chair, feet flat on the floor, back straight but not stiff. Close your eyes or lower your gaze.

Now cross your arms across your body so that each hand is resting gently on the opposite shoulder. Begin to pat your shoulders with alternate movements of your hands; as you breathe in, pat your left shoulder; as you breathe out, pat your right shoulder. Depending on your speed of breathing, you may want to pat left–right on an in-breath, and left–right on an out-breath.

Keep your mind focused on your breath and the sensation of alternate patting for several minutes; allow your out-breath to be longer than your in-breath. When your mind wanders, come back to your breath or the movement in your hands. Come back as many times as your mind wanders, without criticism or judgement.

After about three or four minutes, sit quietly for a minute. Focus on sounds or your breath. Then open your eyes or lift your gaze, and move gently on with whatever you want to do next.

MINDFUL DIGITAL DETOX

We live our lives in an almost permanently 'connected' state. Our phones, tablets, computers and other electronic devices bombard us with a constant stream of stimulus far beyond anything we have evolved to cope with. We click around the internet from topic to topic, from serious news to celebrity gossip, while simultaneously trying to hold conversations with people on apps, emails and texts. Our minds are often over-stimulated, and such engagement does not foster calm or clarity of thinking. Smartphones, while amazing and wonderful, represent a masterclass in distraction. When used mindlessly (without awareness), we are pulled and pushed around like ships on a rough sea, at the mercy of advertisers, body-shamers, the latest fads and fashions. Used wisely, our devices are fantastic servants; used unwisely, they can become merciless masters, always pushing us around and intruding into our lives. Here are some suggestions for engaging mindfully with technology:

- Be mindful of how often you are checking devices for messages, likes, comments, emails, text messages. How often are you obsessively looking at your phone for the next input? Be mindful that smartphones and apps are *designed* to fascinate us and make us spend more and more of our lives looking at them.

- Be aware that your reptilian brain responds to these stimuli in 'threat' mode: each 'ping', each alert, captures your attention and makes it nearly impossible to ignore until you are satisfied that you are safe, that there is no action to take, or that you have fired off a rapid response.

- App creators know that the dopamine 'hit' in your brain (a pleasure-generating neurotransmitter) every time you respond to a like, a message or alert is addictive. It's what keeps us glued to our devices. Their intention is to keep you fixed on your screens for as long as possible, rather than engaged with life around you. The more you click, the more you stick.

- Take seriously the idea of having regular screen detoxes. At least once a week, have a morning or an evening with your devices switched off. Ensure that every night before you go to bed, you switch them off too. Checking devices during the night is a sure sign that they have successfully infiltrated your mind to an excessive extent. There is no need to check emails at 3am. Doing so trains your mind to never switch off and relax; you are stoking anxiety and stress.

- Try not to react immediately to messages and alerts: our reptilian brain typically reacts from a place of threat and we may post things that we later regret. Take time to respond from a more compassionate, considered space.

- When you are talking face-to-face to friends, put your phone away (out of sight – not face-down on the table) so that you can be fully present with that person.

- When you are studying, turn your devices off or shut your email down, so that you can give your full attention to your work. Contrary to popular myth, humans are not good at multitasking: we can only truly focus on one thing at a time. Attempting to do otherwise elevates stress and anxiety hormones and reduces effectiveness.

GRASPING AND AVOIDING

We all want to be happy in life. Yet the way we try to be happy is often, paradoxically, the very thing that drives our unhappiness and anxiety. According to Buddhist thought, there are two equal but opposite tendencies within us all which we deploy in an attempt to find happiness by controlling external circumstances: *grasping* (trying to capture those aspects of life we love) and *avoiding* (trying to steer clear of those aspects of life we find difficult). Our working hypothesis seems to be that if we put enough effort into holding on to what makes us happy (loving relationships, good jobs, success) and into dodging all the bad stuff (illness, unemployment, cheating partners) we will be happy and free from anxiety.

Unfortunately, this approach does not work in the long term. As you may have already discovered – and if not yet, eventually you will – much of life is beyond our control. The reality is that no matter how hard we try to hold on to the good things and shun the bad, life is constantly changing. We inhabit a 'living-dying' world (Brach, 2017); none of us can fully control the social, political and economic situation we have been born into. Relationships (our own, our parents', our friends') can break down, hard-working students fail exams or don't always get the jobs they hope for, we all grow old, everyone we love will die. These are the realities of life, which may seem harsh, but our attempts to avoid these realities (the grasping and avoiding) merely serve to heighten our anxieties. We forget that most challenges we face fall into one of three categories: 1) those we have complete control over; 2) those we have some control over; and 3) those we have no control over. Problems arise when we confront a situation over which we have only some or no control as if we have complete control over it. A common example is the approach to exam results that some students have: 'I must get a first' implies complete control over an outcome, whereas the reality is that you only have some control (how well you study, the questions included on the paper, how well you feel on the day of the exam). In fact, there are very few situations we have complete control over; unless we are able to accept this, the unrealistic thoughts whirling around in our minds unwittingly create additional stress and anxiety for ourselves.

Psychologists are in agreement that there is no pain-free way to avoid anxiety. The harder you try, the worse it gets. The more situations you avoid in order not to feel anxious (making presentations, asking someone on a date, going to a party), the more restricted your life will become: your 'comfort zone' will become your 'misery zone'. The title of a classic self-help book sums up the only way to face anxiety and stop it restricting our lives: *Feel the Fear and Do It Anyway* (Jeffers, 2007). If we see our anxiety as a red light, telling us to 'STOP!', our lives will get smaller and smaller because every new situation we encounter will, thanks to our reptilian brain/threat system, trigger some degree of anxiety. On the other hand, if we turn towards our anxiety and recognise that what we are feeling is what everyone feels, that it is a natural, essential part of our human nature, we can begin to treat ourselves gently, but firmly, and rather than trying to avoid anxiety-provoking situations, learn to see them as opportunities to grow.

Mindfulness can help us to recognise our own avoidance and grasping: our futile attempts to make happiness and comfort permanent. It helps us to recognise our tendency to try to control situations that are not within our control. True mindfulness is not a comfort blanket, something that will, if practised hard enough, make our anxieties disappear. On the contrary, as we become more familiar with our unrealistic and unhelpful thoughts and deepest beliefs about how life *should* be, mindfulness will challenge us to let go of our avoidant/grasping nature, and to embrace life just as it is. Far from being an easy way out of life's problems, mindfulness can, and will, enable you to develop self-and-other compassion as you recognise the challenges in being fully open to life. You come to see that it is only by being fully present to *life-as-it-is* rather than *life-as-you-think-it-should-be* that true, deep confidence emerges, accompanied by a trust in your ability to respond with wisdom to whatever life brings your way.

For Gabriela, the adjustment to a new country and new culture was an enormous challenge which she had completely underestimated. Her threat system was 'on' and stayed that way for much longer than she could have imagined. For her, it was helpful simply to understand some of the physiology of her response to her new situation: while intellectually she could understand the reasons for some of her distress and discomfort, she still had to go through the biological reactions that were triggered by her brain as she adjusted to a 'new normal'. Mindfulness proved to be an important ally in her quest to regain her composure: she found stretches of formal meditation to be soothing and stabilising. With the help of other international students, she came to see that her reactions were not unique but were shared by many others. This enabled her to be more compassionate towards herself and not to fight with the reality of her situation.

QUESTIONS FOR REFLECTION

1. If experiencing anxiety is a normal part of everyone's experience, how are you responding to your own anxieties? With compassion? With anxiety? With depression? Do you hope that somehow you might find a magic way to avoid anxiety? Or are you able to relate to it more gently and more acceptingly?

2. 'My life has been filled with terrible misfortune: most of which never happened' (Michel de Montaigne). Take a moment to reflect on some of the things you have fretted, worried, stressed about in the past. How many of these things have actually happened?

3. Having an anxious thought does not mean it is true. Next time you are in a car, or on a bus, try a thought experiment. Tell yourself: 'We're going to have a puncture.' Repeat that thought over and over and over. See what happens. Does thinking about something make it happen? If not, can you change the way you relate to the anxiety-provoking thoughts your mind produces?

FURTHER READING

Fabrice Midal (2019) *C'est la vie: The French Art of Letting Go*. London: Seven Dials.

A thoughtful plea for us to drop many of our unhelpful attempts to avoid anxiety. The author explores how attempts to attain perfection and control merely serve to increase our unhappiness and anxiety.

Richard Carlson (1997) *Stop Thinking, Start Living: Discover Lifelong Happiness*. Shaftesbury: Element.

The author illustrates clearly how our reaction to our thoughts can ensnare us and keep us from experiencing true happiness. He gives clear, practical tools to emerge from monkey mind with a clearer appreciation of the present moment.

REFERENCES

Brach, T. (2017) The reality of change: embracing this living dying world. Available at: www.youtube.com/watch?v=iKbMNkd3S7Y (accessed 24 January 2019).

Coelho, P. (2013) *Manuscript Found in Accra*. New York, NY: Random House.

Jeffers, S. (2007) *Feel the Fear and Do It Anyway: How to Turn Your Fear and Indecision into Confidence and Action*. London: Vermillion.

'THE BEST TIME
TO PLANT A TREE WAS
TWENTY YEARS AGO.
THE NEXT BEST TIME
IS NOW.,

Chinese proverb
(author unknown)

8
MINDFULNESS
AND PROCRASTINATION

IN THIS CHAPTER YOU WILL:

- explore the common experience of procrastination;

- understand different procrastination styles, and how mindfulness can help you to recognise your own patterns of avoidance;

- learn simple techniques for confronting procrastination – in a self-compassionate rather than self-bullying way;

- appreciate how the practice of formal mindfulness in itself will likely provoke tendencies to procrastinate – and the importance of honesty with yourself;

- understand how making time and space to incorporate mindful pauses into your day can be part of a 'virtuous circle' of commitment to what really matters for you.

Anne is a part-time mature student studying for a Master's in Criminal Psychology. She is holding down a job, has a young daughter who will start school in a year's time and a partner who travels away on business a lot. Although she loves her studies and needs her degree in order to be able to progress in her career, Anne finds juggling the demands of work, home and course intensely challenging. She has had to seek various extensions to deadlines for essays – something she hates doing – and as she looks ahead to the research element of her course, she experiences a kind of dread in her body, wondering how on earth she will find the time to do what needs to be done. The feeling of dread induces in Anne a sense of helplessness, which in turn leads her to ask herself 'What's the point?' just when she could sit down and do half an hour's reading or writing. Instead of doing what she can in the time she has available, Anne finds herself tidying the house, doing some ironing or just sitting in front of a TV programme she doesn't even want to watch – all with a gnawing awareness that she is wasting time, avoiding the things that most need her attention. Anne responds to the pressures of her situation by procrastinating: constantly putting off sitting down to get on with some work. She feels guilty and full of self-reproach. As an undergraduate, Anne worked hard and did well. Now she compares her current performance to those days and feels a kind of despair because she simply does not have the amount of time available that she would really like to focus on her studies. The vicious circle of procrastination is dragging Anne down: the more she puts off doing work, the guiltier she feels, so the more she avoids doing anything to help herself. She is caught up in ruminating thoughts that repeat over and over: 'I'm useless', 'There's no point in starting if I can't do at least two hours' work', which are getting her nowhere.

We all know the feeling. A piece of work that we were told about months ago – and which, we confidently told ourselves, we would have *plenty* of time to complete – is now due in tomorrow and we've barely started to do anything about it. Over the weeks, we've managed to convince ourselves that it really doesn't matter that we haven't begun to do anything meaningful towards getting the piece of work done. But gradually, as time moves rather too quickly by, there is a growing sense of avoidance along with many justifications as to why we haven't tackled something which, in reality, we have had more than enough time to do.

Although Anne's story is quite typical, all of us have a tendency to put things off on a daily basis. Getting up, going to bed, phoning home, taking books back to the library, cleaning our rooms, paying bills; the list goes on. It's as if the desire to *do* something meets an equal and opposite desire to *avoid*. And more often than we'd like to acknowledge, we just happen to find ourselves *doing nothing*.

In their book *It's About Time!*, Dr Linda Sapadin and Jack Maguire identify six common patterns of procrastination (Sapadin and Maguire, 1997). These patterns reflect deeply held personal beliefs and assumptions about who you are, about other people and about the way the world is. It's worth reading their book to familiarise yourself with your own common patterns of procrastination because without awareness, change is impossible. We need to become very familiar with our own thought and behaviour patterns, and the beliefs that underpin them, before we can realistically take steps to change.

Briefly, the six styles of procrastination that Linda and Jack describe are:

1. *The overdoer:* you are someone who, basically, can't say 'no' to the requests that come your way from friends, family or colleagues. And not only do you say 'yes' too often, you even go as far as volunteering to take on tasks you see need doing. You might be the one who always tries to get people organised to stick to a cleaning rota in your house, or who ends up cleaning the kitchen for the umpteenth time after everyone else has simply walked away. You may struggle with being assertive and with recognising your own needs as being at least as important as those of others. Most people who looked at your calendar would think: 'You're doing too much!'

2. *The crisis-maker:* you are someone who has come to rely on the crisis-fuelled adrenalin rush of last-minute attempts to get your work done. You frequently pull all-nighters, consuming energy drinks, or resorting to other kinds of 'uppers' to meet

your deadline. You may sincerely believe that you work best under pressure. But you never actually allow yourself to know what might be possible if you were to plan ahead, and have realistic mini goals on the way to achieving your desired outcomes. There may be an unconscious strategy to avoid giving yourself the time you need to do a task: that way, if you don't do as well as you hoped, you can just tell yourself: 'I was too busy to do that properly; this isn't what I'm *really* capable of.'

3. *The dreamer:* you are someone who tends to drift through life. Somehow, you manage to pass exams, hand in a piece of work which passes (just), but you don't really engage with work. Instead, you prefer to imagine winning the lottery, marrying someone rich, or just having a lucky break. You may feel that 'normal rules' (revising, working hard) don't apply to you; they are for other people. You see yourself as different – special – and just waiting for that big break that will propel you to stardom or riches.

4. *The defier:* you are someone who resents being told what to do. You may unconsciously resist deadlines, preferring instead to hand work in late in order to show your tutor who's boss. If someone gives you a deadline, part of you thinks, 'I'll show them, no one's telling *me* what to do!' As a result, you rarely meet deadlines, you gain a reputation for being 'difficult' or unreliable.

5. *The perfectionist:* you are someone who is basically never satisfied with whatever work you do. When you sit down to write an essay, you continually delete what you've written, only to start over again, and end up doing the same thing. Clearly, this is linked to an overall issue with perfectionism (see Chapter 6) and the fear of not being good enough, or of always feeling that you just need to read one more book or paper, just find one more reference before you can make a start. You make the perfect the enemy of the good and this stops you from focusing on what is possible rather than what is perfect.

6. *The worrier:* it's really hard for you to trust yourself. You always doubt your understanding of what's expected of you in work. When you *do* sit down to work, you find yourself constantly feeling that you need to ask someone else what you're supposed to do, or whether you've understood what the question means. As a result, you spend more time checking things than getting on with what you can do.

Clearly, these 'styles' of procrastination are not stand-alone, discrete phenomena. You probably recognise something of yourself in several descriptions. Nevertheless, my experience of working with students is that the most common procrastination styles are *perfectionist* and *crisis-maker*. Often, these two styles combine to form a toxic mix that leads people to burn out and feel utterly intimidated by whatever deadline they are facing. They end up losing all confidence in themselves to do what they say they will do, and this becomes deeply depressing: 'If I can't even trust myself to do what I said I'll do, what does that say about me?' For Anne, who we met at the beginning of the chapter, struggling with so many different areas of life, there is a tendency to be something of an overdoer. However, she also has an inclination to be a perfectionist as she compares her current situation with how things used to be as an undergraduate and is unable to accept that those days are over, and what was possible then may not be realistic now.

Mindfulness, as we've seen in previous chapters, means accepting whatever thoughts, feelings and behaviours we observe in ourselves without criticism. *Stopping, observing, accepting*: taking a mindful pause when we recognise that we are engaged in avoidant behaviour such as procrastination. Our natural tendency is to *turn away* from our experience when it is painful or other than what we think it 'should' be. One therapist, Karen Horney, refers to a state of mind she calls the 'tyranny of the should' (Hancox, 2014): a good way of summarising the experience of feeling burdened by a version of ourselves, others and the world, which stops us from accepting things as they are rather than as we imagine they ought to be. This turning away can take many forms, including alcohol, drugs, sleep, sex, food and exercise: anything that has avoidance as its motivation. By contrast, with mindfulness we *turn towards* our thoughts, feelings and behaviour, and this can take courage and determination. Remember: *mindfulness is simple, but not easy.*

Mindfulness invites us to become really familiar with what is going on inside us: not only as a means to an end of engaging in more helpful and healthful choices, but also simply in order to be able to approach with compassion the emotional and behavioural patterns that have built up over many years, often for complex reasons. Our tendency, when we glimpse unhelpful thoughts, feelings and behaviours within ourselves, is to be harshly self-critical: 'What an idiot!'; 'I must try harder!'; 'I'm such a loser'. Mindfulness asks us to develop awareness *and* self-compassion; to adopt a new stance towards ourselves and to have faith that this can open up a gentler, more realistic way of being.

MINDFUL EXERCISE

Take a sheet of paper, or open a new document on your computer. Write down very quickly the most difficult thing that you are putting off in your life at the moment. It can be a piece of work, a difficult conversation, paying a bill, getting help or advice, etc.

For a few minutes, simply allow yourself to look at what you have written and just notice whatever associations that spontaneously arise. Let your mind produce the typical worrying, self-critical thoughts that occur when you are contemplating taking meaningful action over this issue. Allow yourself to *really see* or *hear these thoughts*. Don't push them away. You might write them down, or speak them out loud: 'I'm useless'; 'I'll never be any different'; 'This is a waste of time'. As you do this, from time to time close your eyes and identify any areas of your body that feel tense, tight, hot or cold. Allow yourself to become familiar with your physical reaction to the idea of taking meaningful action. Perhaps consider whether you see any worrying, perfectionistic or crisis-maker thoughts arising, such as, 'I've left it too late; whatever I do now is bound to be rubbish' or 'This is just too much, I'm going to watch some YouTube videos and calm myself down'.

Now, spend five minutes completing these sentences, based on what you have just observed: 'I think ...' and 'I feel ...'. Try to write whatever you notice

● ● ● ●

and observe, without censuring and without judging. Some examples of this might include:

- 'I think that I'm just not ever going to change. I'll never be a person who gets work done on time, I'll always be someone who puts things off to the last moment.'

- 'I think this is all too much for me. I think I shouldn't be even trying to do this. All I can think of is escaping and stopping these awful feelings.'

- 'I feel a heavy weight in my chest, a real burden on my shoulders and my heart beating quite fast.'

- 'I feel nothing: as I sit here, my body feels numb.'

Be very aware, too, of the self-critical thoughts that accompany your experience. Simply notice the words, tone and feel of those thoughts. Observe these repetitive thought-loops in your brain – criticising you, condemning you, putting you down. Your own internal bully.

You are now much more consciously aware of some of your internal processes and patterns, thoughts and feelings about what happens for you when you avoid doing things that are important to you. This may not feel like much progress, but what you have done is demonstrate a willingness to *turn towards* your experience of procrastination, and you are beginning to see that there is far more to it than simply being lazy or lacking in motivation. There are 'good reasons' for avoidance, and most of these 'good reasons' are fear-based, driven by that reptilian part of your brain that may experience deadlines as a threat – something to avoid at all costs.

TECHNIQUES FOR DEALING WITH PROCRASTINATION

Mindfulness provides a way to become familiar with our own patterns of avoidance. This is a crucial first step on the journey towards compassionate re-engagement with what *needs* to be done, and what you *want* to get done. An important way to develop self-compassion is to take great care when you tune in to that inner voice that provides a running commentary on how you are doing, and to respond with compassion and kindness if it becomes an internal bully. Let's see an example of how this might work:

Internal bully   You'll never get that work done! You know you won't. Just face it, you're just not organised enough and you never will be.

Internal friend   It's true that I struggle with organising my work, but this is not easy for anyone. Work at this level is meant to be demanding and so it's natural for me to feel anxiety about tackling it. But I don't need to add to the challenge by putting myself down. I will do what I can, and accept that I may need help. I am not a loser – I am learning to deal with things that most people find challenging and daunting. That's OK; I will be as kind as possible to myself while I am doing this.

Responding with compassion takes practice and commitment, and if the internal bully is very strong, you may need help from a friend or professional to really strengthen your internal friend. None of us respond well to persistent criticism: it saps our motivation and confidence. We all need to be encouraged and praised for the effort we make to achieve our goals: we all need to be our own best cheerleaders. Developing the voice of the internal friend is *not* the same as positive thinking, which might simply be unrealistic thinking; for example, 'I *will* write 5,000 words today'. Instead, it is like the voice of a caring parent towards a scared child – acknowledging their fears and reassuring them that it *is* safe to go to bed because there are no monsters in the wardrobe.

APPROACHING RATHER THAN AVOIDING WORK

A very common pitfall when approaching academic work, or any other challenging situation, is failing to break it down into manageable chunks. There's a rather graphic question to illustrate this: 'How do you eat an elephant?' Answer: 'In bite-sized chunks.' Now, I'm not suggesting that anyone should eat an elephant, but the point is that any task as big as, say, a dissertation, or revising for an exam, or preparing a presentation can't be tackled all in one go. It must be broken down into bite-sized pieces that are then 'eaten' in reasonable portions.

When I was doing my own doctorate, the most helpful technique that enabled me to complete it were SMART goals. In fact, it's no exaggeration to say that without this technique, I doubt I would have ever finished, because at times the whole project seemed so massive and unachievable. There are many good guides to using SMART goals, but very briefly SMART stands for:

Specific

Measurable

Achievable

Realistic

Time-limited

Each part of the acronym is important when tackling anything other than small, easily accomplished tasks. So, for instance, rather than a vague, unhelpful and demotivating thought such as 'Must do some work this weekend', I learned to write weekly SMART goals such as: 'Write 500 words as part of draft literature review by 2pm on Saturday.' This is specific (500 words – literature review), measurable and achievable (because I set the goal on the preceding Monday), realistic (I didn't set myself a massive 2,000-word goal) and time-limited (2pm on Saturday).

Getting into the habit of setting weekly and monthly SMART goals has the potential to transform your working patterns. However, until you are familiar with the process of setting these goals, I recommend that you ask someone to help you do this: to assess the overall piece of work that you need to achieve, and to help you break it up into those bite-sized chunks. Eventually, you'll be able to do this for yourself. The 'realistic' part is so important and many students are hopelessly over-ambitious about what they can or should achieve within a certain time-frame. It's so much better to set small goals that you can achieve, rather than large goals that you miss. Success breeds success, and you will develop confidence in your ability to manage work by being able to tick several small goals off your list, rather than failing to achieve a huge one. I also suggest that you make yourself accountable to another person once you have written your goals; someone who is not too easily fobbed off if you turn around and say, 'Well, I know I was supposed to be working but I just didn't feel like it'. Someone who will ask some tough questions about why you didn't achieve your goals – but of course, not someone who will start to bully you if you slip up.

Another helpful tip when you feel hopelessly stuck and unable to face what you have to do is 'the ten-minute rule'. This is very simple, and means that you say to yourself: 'I really, really don't feel like doing any work, I just want to go out and forget about it. *But* I will do ten minutes' worth of work and *then* if I still feel like avoiding it, I will.' You make a commitment that for ten minutes you will do what needs doing. And only then will you decide whether to keep going or stop. Quite often, you'll find, after ten minutes of genuinely engaging with your task, you'll feel rather differently about it and want to carry on: motivation and interest don't come *before* the task, they come *after* you start it. However, after ten minutes if you still feel like going out, that's OK.

Mindfulness practice in and of itself is also a key part of facing up to and dealing with procrastination. The discipline of formal mindfulness practice, preferably each day but at least three times a week, develops your confidence and discipline, along with self-compassion as you observe over and over again the way your mind tends to get distracted and entangled in self-bullying, unhelpful thoughts.

MINDFUL EXERCISE

Commit to a set period of daily, formal mindfulness practice for the next two weeks. I strongly suggest that this period should not be too long, but not too short either: fifteen minutes is ideal. Commit to a period of time which, for you, is SMART. If at all possible, choose the same time each day to practise: usually, first thing in the morning is best, but any time when you are generally free and not likely to fall asleep is fine. Just try not to be surrounded by too much noise or activity: you might find a place where you won't be disturbed such as a park, a sacred space such as a church, mosque or temple, or – more conveniently – your own bedroom (using ear plugs if necessary).

Keep a simple journal recording your practice: it can be as easy as putting a tick on a calendar every time you sit.

Be prepared for your procrastination habits to very powerfully exert themselves as you go through the two-week period. One of the hardest aspects of formal mindfulness – if not *the* hardest – is commitment. Notice the thoughts and feelings that creep into your mind when it's your time to practise. 'Can't be bothered', 'Too tired', 'What's the point?', 'I haven't got time today', 'I'll do it later', and so on. See if it's possible to *expect* these thoughts, and to be prepared for them. As with your academic work, relying on *feeling motivated* to practise mindfulness will not get you very far at all. Feeling motivated is a luxury that may or may not manifest itself very often: what counts is a willingness to turn up and practise regularly. And the same is true of academic work: feeling motivated is a poor emotion to rely on – you won't get through a tough degree course by waiting to feel motivated: remember the ten-minute rule.

This practice – daily, short mindfulness meditation – can become an anchor for you: a reminder that you *can* commit to something that you may not always feel like doing. There *will* be times when you miss your practice (just as there will be times when you don't achieve all your SMART goals). What counts is not seeing one or two missed sessions as failure, or an indication that you are not cut out for meditation or academic work: *this is the practice*. And, holding that awareness, compassionately bring yourself to sit on your cushion, in your chair or on the floor and – rather in the way you brush your teeth every day without asking yourself whether you feel like it or not – bring formal mindfulness into your daily life. As you develop your mindfulness practice over a period of days and weeks, see in this your ability to tackle academic work in a compassionate, mindful, SMART way.

QUESTIONS FOR REFLECTION

1. As you seek to try out some regular times of mindfulness meditation practice, or if you have tried to do this previously, what kind of excuses are likely to come up with in order to avoid this? Do these excuses reflect your main procrastination style?

2. Being clear about your reasons for putting time aside to practise mindful meditation is important. Without a sense of *why* you are making this commitment, you are less likely to keep going. Your reasons will evolve, but today, now – what is your deepest intention and hope for practising mindfulness?

3. 'If I can't trust myself to do what I say I will do – who *can* I trust?' (Perry, 2002). How might building a strong commitment to mindfulness strengthen your sense of confidence in your ability to achieve the things that are important to you?

FURTHER READING

Gregg Krech (2014) *The Art of Taking Action: Lessons from Japanese Psychology*. Monkton Boro, VT: ToDo Institute.

Insights from Eastern philosophy into how our minds so often lead us to avoid what most matters to us, and gentle, practical tips for taking meaningful action.

Robert Maurer (2004) *One Small Step to Change Your Life: The Kaizen Way*. New York: Workman Publishing.

Often, when we think of making change, we 'thing big' – and then fail. Here, the author explains the Japanese concept of *kaizen* where we learn to overcome resistance by taking tiny, consistent steps towards our ultimate goal.

REFERENCES

Hancox, D. (2014) The tyranny of the should. Available at: https://corecounselling.ca/the-tyranny-of-the-should/ (accessed 24 January 2019).

Perry, A. (2002) *Isn't It about Time? How to Overcome Procrastination and Get On with Your Life*. Duffield: Worth Publishing.

Sapadin, L. and Maguire, J. (1997) *It's about Time!: The 6 Styles of Procrastination and How to Overcome Them*. Penguin.

'**ONE CANNOT THINK WELL**, LOVE WELL, SLEEP WELL, **IF ONE HAS NOT DINED WELL**.'

Virginia Woolf, *A Room of One's Own* (1929)

9

MINDFULNESS

AND SELF-CARE

IN THIS CHAPTER YOU WILL:

- explore the importance of self-care to your physical and mental wellbeing;

- recognise the limitations of your ability to function well without attending to food, exercise and sleep;

- consider what studying and working mindfully might look like for you;

- discover how mindfulness can help you acknowledge and attend to your fundamental physical needs.

Asaf has arrived at university full of enthusiasm for the opportunity to study and meet new people. He has big hopes for his future and hopes to set up his own business when he graduates. He loves the excitement of exploring a new city, and of making new friends. He's been looking forward to leaving home and having some freedom and independence for the first time in his life. Yet, despite his eagerness to get the most out of every opportunity and his positive attitude, he is getting tired, putting on weight, and generally starting to feel lacking in confidence. At home, he has always been super-confident, a popular person at school and within his large extended family. He can't understand why he is now feeling so unwell and unable to cope. He is struggling to keep up with lectures and feels he is falling behind other students on his course: his self-confidence has taken a real knock. The reality is that Asaf has underestimated the impact of leaving home and the pressures of starting to look after himself for the first time. He is not used to cooking or managing a budget, and he has stopped playing football because he wasn't accepted onto the university team, something he found humiliating and frustrating. Although he is very able and personable, Asaf is ignoring the fundamentals of self-care and is suffering as a result. His diet is haphazard, consisting mainly of take-away food or sandwiches and his sleep pattern is all over the place: sometimes he is in bed for ten, other days it is three in the morning before he puts his light off. He has also pretty much stopped getting outside to exercise; the less he does, the less he feels like doing anything. Faced with the responsibility of looking after himself for the first time in his life, Asaf is slowly starting to realise just how much his parents did for him when he was living at home and how difficult it seems to manage simple things such as shopping, cooking and budgeting. Without the basics being taken care of for him, Asaf is struggling to keep on top of the things that would enable him to function well and healthily.

I once heard about a student who, on starting university, decided that she was going to find an easy, stress-free way of catering for herself. No preparing fresh food or chopping vegetables for her. She went to the supermarket and bought a month's supply of instant flavoured noodles: easy to prepare, just add boiling water and stir. Not surprisingly, after a couple of weeks, she was starting to feel extremely unwell. She was suffering from headaches, poor sleep and a rather nasty bout of constipation. It wasn't until she went home for a weekend and was enjoying home-cooking again that she realised the truth that woman cannot live by instant flavoured noodles alone.

Sleeping, eating and exercising are the three legs of the 'stool' of wellbeing (see Figure 9.1). When students come for counselling, we often begin by exploring how things are going in these three basic areas of life. Very often we discover that one or more of these needs is causing problems. Sleep is typically a major concern: difficulties falling asleep, staying asleep or waking early. As exam pressure builds, there can be a sense there is not enough time to prepare healthy food or to take time out for exercise. Unsurprisingly, as one of these areas begins to falter, the others follow suit: lack of exercise affects sleep; comfort eating or avoiding food kicks in ... The result is a strong feeling of being out of sorts, depressed, lethargic and generally under par. Consequently, studying and working are suffering, sometimes quite badly.

Figure 9.1   Three foundations for wellbeing

PHYSICAL SELF-CARE: THE FOUNDATION FOR MENTAL WELLBEING

In the 1940s, American psychologist Abraham Maslow identified different levels of human motivation for getting certain needs met which he believed are universal across all cultures (Maslow, 1943). These levels of motivation strongly influence our focus at any given time, with the higher levels of motivation coming into play only when the lower levels have been sufficiently satisfied. From his work emerged the well-known 'hierarchy of needs' pyramid, giving a good visual representation of the different levels of motivation, and emphasising the importance of a solid foundation of physiological needs that must be adequately met before we can focus on other, higher-level needs.

If we look at the pyramid in Figure 9.2, we see at the top 'self-actualisation', which includes things like self-expression, self-determination and other abstract needs important to students such as creativity and critical thinking. Indeed, we could say that much of what is deemed important to 'success' as a student involves the ability to engage with motivations towards the top of the pyramid. As students, you are expected to be motivated to pursue challenging academic work. However, the ability to do so is, in fact, highly dependent on sufficient of the 'lower' needs being adequately met.

Right at the bottom of the pyramid, the strong base upon which all other needs can be addressed, sits 'physiological needs'. This makes obvious sense. It's very hard to engage your mind in intellectual work if you are worried about having enough money to live on, if your accommodation is not good, or if you are not eating well. I know from first-hand experience that if you are living in noisy halls where your sleep is regularly disturbed, or if you find yourself living with people you don't get on with and around whom you feel anxiety, this will inevitably impinge on your ability to study well. I once heard a female refugee describe how, before leaving her home country where all her fundamental needs

Figure 9.2   Maslow's hierarchy of needs

had been met, she had been starting a PhD; now, alone and destitute, surrounded by a different culture and language, the only concern she had was to find a bed for the night. Basic needs must be sufficiently met before you can proceed to produce your best work, and feel comfortable and confident in your student environment. This doesn't mean that you must have every need (or, importantly, *want*) satisfied. It simply means that there is a level of basic needs that cannot be ignored before you are able to attend to more abstract needs.

Mindfulness provides us with a very helpful way to be in touch with our needs, to be able to assess which areas of life we may need to make changes in and focus on in order to function at our best. Practising mindfulness enables us to step out of our thinking minds, to come into our bodies, and to hear and acknowledge what they may be telling us. For instance, I have seen many students who, when practising formal sitting meditation, fall asleep very quickly. Rather than berating themselves for dropping off, I encourage them to recognise that they may simply need more sleep if they are to function well in their studies and social life. If you too find that you begin to nod off as soon as you start to practise formal mindfulness meditation, please don't be too self-critical: just acknowledge that this may be your body asking you to rest more often and to address your sleep behaviour. Again, it is sometimes only when a person gives themselves some space and time to reconnect with their bodily experience that they may notice tension, aches and pains which need care and attention.

MIND AND BODY: THE ILLUSION OF SEPARATION

The sixteenth-century French philosopher René Descartes famously wrote: '*Je pense, donc je suis*' – 'I think, therefore I am' (Descartes, 1637). Some see this statement as representative of a tendency in Western culture to denigrate the body at the expense of the mind. Thinking, reason and science may be seen as 'higher', more noble, than physical experience. We might argue that some religious traditions, too, have seen the body as a source of sin, uncleanliness and something to overcome rather than to honour. These apparently conflicting understandings of how mind and body relate to each other are actually very unhelpful. In reality, of course, it is impossible to separate mind and body, though as students you may find that your course curricula encourage more development of mind than body.

Through mindfulness, we are invited to 'come home' to our breath and our bodies, to consciously and deliberately tune in to what is going on there, noticing many subtle and changing sensations which, most of the time, simply sit beneath our conscious awareness. The following exercise is a gentle way of acknowledging that, as well as being a thinking, analytical mind, you are a physical body with physical needs. As always, there is no necessity for self-criticism or judgement when you engage in this exercise; instead, the invitation is to be curious about what you discover and to simply notice whether you begin to identify any underlying needs that you would like to address.

MINDFUL EXERCISE

Try to allow fifteen to twenty minutes for this exercise. Find a quiet space where you can sit and not be disturbed.

Make yourself comfortable on a chair, or a meditation mat or stool. Take a few moments to simply settle; adjust your posture so that you are unlikely to experience any physical discomfort throughout the exercise. If you do experience discomfort, it's fine to gently and mindfully move your body so that you don't experience pain. But try not to keep shifting positions: the more you move, the more you will want to keep on moving, which can be distracting.

Now, take a few slow, deep breaths. Make your out-breath slightly longer than your in-breath. Nice and deep, letting go of tension and stress as you breathe out. Do this for a few moments, and then, on an out-breath, either close your eyes or allow your gaze to fall onto a spot about two metres in front of you on the floor.

And now allow your breathing to return to its normal rhythm; not forcing it, not trying to control it or change it in any way.

Now, bring your full attention to your breath – following each in-breath and each out-breath as completely as you can. Take a few moments to identify where in your body you feel your breathing most vividly: In your chest? Your stomach? Your nose? Your mouth? When you find the place where your breath feels clearest, gently rest your attention there for a few moments. Recognise that your breath is an anchor to the present moment – a means whereby you can re-establish your awareness of your body and, for a short

● ● ● ●

time, shift your focus away from your ever-thinking, monkey mind. Simply follow the sensations of breathing now for a few minutes, and when your mind wanders, just come back to your breath as many times as you need to.

After a few minutes, gently redirect your attention to any sensations that are most vivid in your body. It could perhaps be simply the feeling of the weight of your body pressing down on the chair or stool or sensations in your feet where they make contact with the floor. Wherever you recognise sensations, allow yourself to acknowledge them now; some may be pleasant, some may be unpleasant and some may simply be neutral. Observe wherever in your body you sense movement: tingling, warmth, pulsing, vibration. Whatever you discover, just allow it to be as it is; don't try to change anything or make any particular feelings happen.

And now, scan through your entire body, bringing your attention to each part of the body in turn; not *thinking about* your body but instead *feeling it* from within.

Start at the top of your head: your scalp, your forehead, your eyes, your cheeks, your jaw, your tongue – what do you notice here? Sensations, temperature, anything that stands out? Or nothing in particular? There's no right or wrong, just taking in whatever feelings are already here.

After that, move your attention to your neck and your shoulders: shoulders are a place where we often hold a lot of tension. Allow your shoulders to relax. Allow your attention to penetrate the top of your shoulders and simply register any sensations that are already there. Notice any feelings that there are in this part of your body, in your neck and throat. Notice when you swallow and how your throat moves when you do so.

Now focus on your torso: your chest, your rib-cage, your back, your stomach. Notice the gentle movements here as you continue to breathe. Just notice. Don't try to change anything or create anything different or special. Allow whatever is here to be here. Note also any more subtle sensations from within your body: your stomach, your heart beating, small movements of feeling within you. Just observe, notice and allow.

Now notice all and any feelings in your arms and hands. Notice the length of your arms and the weight of your hands resting in your lap or on your knees. Again, don't think about your hands and arms, but simply sense them from within. Notice any vibration or warmth in the palms of your hands. Perhaps notice the feeling where your elbows bend and sense the bones of your elbows under your skin. Simply allowing whatever feelings you discover to be here.

And when your mind wanders away onto other things, accept this as normal and nothing to worry about. This is not a competition. There's no right or wrong. No one to judge you. Simply refocus on your body as much as you can for these few moments. If you notice any self-critical thoughts or any self-congratulatory thoughts, recognise them as just thoughts and allow them to float past like clouds in the sky.

Bring your attention to any sensations in your pelvic region: the weight of your body pressing down, the way your body bends here, and any internal sensations that are present.

Down into your legs and feet: feel the length of your legs, the sense of where they bend at the knees, and the feelings in your feet where they touch the floor. Notice the touch of clothes against skin and any other sensations such as vibrations or warmth within your legs and feet.

Finally, expand your focus and allow your attention to take in the whole of your body, sitting here, breathing. For the next few moments, tune in to any sensations as they arise at any point in your body, or follow your breath in and out; and then, when you are ready, gently open your eyes, or lift your gaze and come back into the space around you.

Take a few moments to sit and process whatever came up for you during this exercise:

- Were there any parts of your body that felt particularly tense, or where there is pain? Or did your body feel quite neutral with no particular feelings standing out for you this time?

- Did you feel very drowsy – did you actually fall asleep?

- Did your mind wander a lot? Or were you focused and alert throughout?

There is no right or wrong; you are simply witnessing the unfolding story within your body and, over time, recognising the messages, hints and reminders that your body sends you so that you can be fully in tune with your needs. If you consistently fall asleep whenever you sit to meditate, you may be in need of more sleep, or you may need to meditate at another time of day when you are more alert. If there is constant tension somewhere, you may need to find a way to release this tension through exercise, massage or relaxation exercises. If there is any other, more acute pain, you may wish to talk to your doctor about this.

LISTEN TO THE AUDIO CLIP AT
https://study.sagepub.com/mindfulness

MINDFUL EATING, SLEEPING AND EXERCISING – AND STUDYING

As you read in Chapter 3 where the difference between formal and informal mindfulness practice is discussed, paying attention to eating can be a wonderful way to gently bring more mindfulness into your life. The whole process of shopping for food, preparing it, cooking and eating, can be done with barely any awareness of what you are doing or, alternatively, it can be done with great attention and appreciation and as a way of tuning in to your physical senses.

Our bodies need food to survive and they preferably need good food on a regular basis. We can, for short periods of time, exist on very little or sub standard food. However, we will definitely suffer cognitive problems and start to feel bloated or weak if we are not taking in good nourishment. It can be a real challenge to eat and drink well as a student, perhaps on a limited budget, possibly faced with shopping and cooking for the first time. Nevertheless, three meals and three snacks a day, and avoiding as much processed, fast-food and sugar as possible, are a basis for overall good mental and physical health. You can perhaps suggest cooking together with friends or make sure that you choose healthy options from campus canteens as much as possible. Keep chips and pizza for occasional weekend treats.

It is also similar with exercise: our basic physiological needs must be adequately met if we are not to suffer unintended consequences of inactivity. Our bodies have not evolved to sit for long hours in front of computer and television screens, or scrunched up over books in the library. We need to move, to get our circulation going, to breathe fresh air. Our brains are not computers: when you study, it isn't a question of 'more in – more out'; rather, it is a question of quality over quantity. It's easy to fool yourself (and others) that you're 'studying' when, in fact, you may simply be sat in front of books with your mind engaged elsewhere. Pushing yourself to work harder and longer will eventually take you beyond the point of diminishing returns where the gains for each additional half hour of 'work' become less and less. Time out for exercise is not the opposite of working; regular breaks for movement and fresh air give your brain time to process what you are learning and to come up with new ideas and questions that can immeasurably improve the quality of your study. When I was doing my doctorate, one of my biggest and most significant breakthroughs came when I was out on a bike ride and not consciously doing any work at all.

Finally, sleep is a crucial element in our overall wellbeing. Long periods of insomnia can wreak havoc with our health and drag us down quite seriously. Many students experience disturbed sleep which, while not necessarily meeting criteria for diagnosed insomnia, can nevertheless make studying and socialising feel more challenging. There is plenty of advice about sleeping available on the internet or from your GP, but some key factors include:

- Aim for a regular bedtime, at least on weekdays.
- Avoid caffeine for at least six hours before bedtime (including fizzy drinks and tea).
- Ensure that you make time to wind down before bed rather than going straight from work or socialising to trying to sleep – take time to do a relaxation exercise, listen to some quiet music or have a warm bath or shower.
- Avoid looking at screens in the hour before you go to bed and make sure that your bedroom is as comfortable as possible – window open if at all realistic so that you are breathing fresh air throughout the night.

Eating well and exercising are also fundamental to sleeping well. As mentioned above, food, exercise and sleep are closely interconnected and a deficit in one area will likely have a knock-on effect in each of the others.

MINDFUL EXERCISE

Allow yourself to conduct a compassionate audit of your life in each of the three areas mentioned above: food, exercise and sleep.

On a piece of paper or a computer file, draw up a table with three columns and four rows, as shown in Table 9.1.

Fill in the boxes with your own feelings and thoughts about these areas of your life. It's very easy to feel self-critical and to start labelling yourself: 'I'm a slob' or 'I'm useless at managing my food intake'. Try, as far as possible, to simply notice such criticisms without letting your mind create an entire story about you based on them.

● ● ● ●

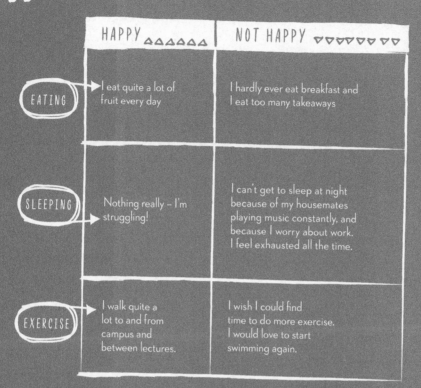

HAPPY △△△△△△	NOT HAPPY ▽▽▽▽▽▽ ▽▽
EATING → I eat quite a lot of fruit every day	I hardly ever eat breakfast and I eat too many takeaways
SLEEPING → Nothing really – I'm struggling!	I can't get to sleep at night because of my housemates playing music constantly, and because I worry about work. I feel exhausted all the time.
EXERCISE → I walk quite a lot to and from campus and between lectures.	I wish I could find time to do more exercise. I would love to start swimming again.

Table 9.1   Mindful audit

Now, gently and compassionately, allow yourself to come up with an intention for yourself in each of these areas. This could take the form of a goal (something you can tick off a list when you've achieved it) or a value (a guiding principle you will seek to apply to this area of life as far as possible). For example:

- Food: I would like to start eating breakfast every day: I want to have good-quality cereal and fruit before I leave the flat.

- Exercise: While I'm walking about campus, I will bring my full attention to the experience rather than rushing. I'll take a slightly longer route to and from halls so that I really get a good walk at least twice a day.

- Sleep: During the week, I'll aim to be in bed for 10.45pm and start winding down about 10pm. I'd like to listen to music and have a cup of herbal tea before I get into bed.

If you prefer, you can do this exercise by creating a mind-map. Get a large piece of paper and different coloured pens or pencils. For each of the areas (food, sleep, exercise) simply draw a large circle, and then draw a line out from the circle to other circles where you note down what feels OK, what you'd like to change and your intention.

Setting goals and intentions are definitely not intended to be guilt inducing and I would encourage you to come up with goals or principles that are as gentle as possible. None of us is ignorant of what we *should* do in order to be as healthy as possible, but often our sense of failure prevents us from taking any meaningful action at all. The Japanese concept of *kaizen* (making small, sometimes tiny, improvements rather than striving for massive change) is helpful here. If you are really struggling with exercise, for example, a tiny change might simply be to imagine yourself exercising. From there, to mindfully walk the length of your room, and then your street, and so on. This is a chance to bring your mindful self-compassion to these three key areas of life and to take small, consistent steps towards behaviours that will meet the fundamental needs which Maslow identified as so important to our wellbeing.

HOW SELF-CARE ENHANCES STUDYING

With enough of your basic needs met, then, what does studying and working mindfully look like? When you are able to focus your attention on coursework, revising, or being on placement, what difference does mindfulness make? I would suggest that mindfulness does make a big difference *before*, *during* and *after* any periods of study.

Before you start to work, the practice of mindfulness can enable you to re centre, to start from a firm foundation of values and intentions. Rather than mindlessly starting to work without clear goals, taking time to establish clear SMART objectives (see Chapter 8) and deciding what is a realistic time-frame for your work can make a huge difference. Taking time to pause before you start can help you to recognise unhelpful thoughts about what your work *should* be like (easy, perfect) and what you *should* be like (more intelligent, less stressed) and to step back from those thoughts and simply observe them. Equally, mindfulness can help you to recognise when you are being too soft on yourself ('I can't be bothered to work, I'll do it later') and again, step back from those thoughts and recognise that each small 'brick in the wall' of study really does matter.

During a period of study, taking mindful breaks can help to keep you on track. Perhaps every half hour, you can simply stand up and practise mindful breathing and walking for a couple of minutes. Retune to your breath and body; noticing what is there. Are you thirsty? Hungry? Sleepy? Anxious? What do you *need*? Allow your gaze to shift to the far distance, give your eyes a break. Notice any thoughts about your work that are around, and acknowledge any unhelpful thoughts ('I'm hopeless at this!', 'I'll never get this done for the deadline, I might as well give up now') and see those thoughts as *just* thoughts. And then return to your task.

After studying, taking a few moments to sit quietly, tuning into your breathing, sounds, sights, aromas and sensations to bring you back into the present moment, rather than rushing onto whatever comes next. Remember, mindfulness is about waking up to more and more of your life through your physical senses. You may recognise strong emotions such as anxiety, worry, joy, elation; allow yourself to simply experience those feelings without getting caught up in dramatic storylines created by your thinking mind. There are no good or bad feelings; some may be pleasant, some may be unpleasant. In mindfulness, we are learning to compassionately allow our physical feelings to come and go without getting tangled up in an emotional story about what those feelings signify.

One very important point about study is to get the balance between effort and relaxation as right as possible for yourself. This balance will be different for everyone, but it's really helpful to have a basic framework for study. For example, you may decide that working for six hours a day – two hours in the morning, two in the afternoon and two in the evening – for six days a week will give you adequate time to complete all your studying. This will then enable you to have one day a week completely free from formal study; instead, you can relax, guilt-free, in the knowledge that by sticking to your schedule you will always achieve your work-goals. Can you establish such a schedule for yourself? And can you integrate mindfulness into and around that schedule? Even short periods of formal and informal mindfulness practice can make a big difference to how you experience your working, studying life. Don't underestimate the impact of taking ten minutes out to reconnect with your environment and your body: practised regularly, mindful breaks can make a huge difference to your experience of being a student.

Asaf joined a mindfulness group at his college – at first simply because he thought it might be a way to meet new people. After spending some time practising the mindful exercise where he scanned through his body, he became much more aware of just how tired he was and how he was depriving himself of sleep and then eating sugary snacks to try to make up for a loss of energy. He also recognised more deeply the reality that adapting to a new environment was more difficult than he had anticipated, and that not being selected for the university football team had been a major blow to his self-esteem. This awareness, and accompanying self-compassion, was key to beginning to develop a more self-caring way of being. With awareness came a greater sense of being able to make informed choices. Of course, he didn't always choose the healthy option, but he was able to understand more of what lay behind other decisions. And he was able to acknowledge that he needed some additional study skills support in order to benefit from his course. He spoke to his tutor, who arranged for him to meet with the mental health advisers at his college where he was able to begin the process of putting that support in place.

The practice of mindfulness in itself encourages us to stay connected to our bodies and our senses. In a fundamental way, mindfulness is *all about* waking up to our physical senses and coming out of our thinking minds. We cannot ignore our physical needs and expect to work well or to feel good about ourselves. I know that for some students, the whole issue of physical needs is a thorny one. There are some students who struggle to allow themselves to eat properly, starving themselves or stuck in a binge–vomit cycle. Others, for example, have given up on their bodies and exercise, feeling that the only solution to their low self-esteem is plastic surgery. The cultivation of deep self-compassion must go hand-in-hand with all mindfulness practices, but once again, I urge you, if you are struggling with self-hatred or addictions, to seek professional help. Mindfulness can encourage awareness of body and of needs; sometimes, we must also seek support as we become more sensitive to how we are working against our own best interests, using food or exercise in unhelpful ways.

QUESTIONS FOR REFLECTION

1. How seriously do you take your physical needs, as fundamental to your success as a student? Is there any unhelpful division between mind and body in terms of what you prioritise for self-care?

2. Mindfulness bridges the gap between mind and body. What does this statement mean for you?

3. When you are studying or taking an exam, how might you incorporate short mindful breaks into that effort?

FURTHER READING

Jan Chozen Bays (2017) *Mindful Eating: A Guide to Rediscovering a Healthy and Joyful Relationship with Food*. Boulder, CO: Shambhala.

A warm and helpful guide to help re-evaluate they ways in which you may be using food to deal with emotional issues. Supportive and with excellent guided meditations.

Danny Penman (2016) *The Art of Breathing*. London: HQ Publishing.

This small book will help you to understand the centrality of breathing to the practice of mindfulness. The author helps us to see how our breath is a wonderful means by which we can retune to a deeper appreciation of the whole of life.

REFERENCES

Descartes, R. (1637) *Discourse on the Method of Rightly Conducting One's Reason and of Seeking Truth in the Sciences*. Available at: www.earlymoderntexts.com/authors/descartes (accessed 4 January 2019).

Maslow, A. (1943) A theory of human motivation. *Psychological Review*, 50, 370–96.

Woolf, V. (1929) *A Room of One's Own*. London: Hogarth Press.

'**WANDERER,**
YOUR FOOTSTEPS ARE THE ROAD,
AND NOTHING MORE;
WANDERER, THERE IS NO ROAD,
THE ROAD IS MADE BY WALKING.

BY WALKING ONE MAKES THE ROAD,

AND UPON GLANCING BEHIND ONE SEES THE
PATH THAT NEVER WILL BE TROD AGAIN.
WANDERER, THERE IS NO ROAD –
ONLY WAKES UPON THE SEA. '

Antonio Machado, Proverbs
and Songs 29 (1912)

10
MINDFULNESS
AND
THE FUTURE

IN THIS CHAPTER YOU WILL:

- explore how anxiety about life after studies is a common experience for many students;

- understand how your search for meaning and purpose can become self-inhibiting;

- consider how values rather than goals may be more helpful guides in life;

- see how mindfulness can help you to let go of unhelpful stories about your future;

Jasminder is in her final year at university. She's been so intent on doing well in her studies that she's given little time to thinking beyond finals. But now, as the date for leaving full-time education draws closer, she is aware of a growing feeling of anxiety. Exams will soon be over; everyone in her house will be moving away, people she's come to know really well over the last three years: all that socialising and support will be gone. Jas knows that she's left it late to start applying for jobs. Most of the big recruiters have closed their graduate entry schemes for this year but earlier on she just didn't feel able to devote the time and energy to getting a CV done, filling in applications, going to the careers service. More fundamentally, Jas doesn't have a clear idea of what she wants to do with her life. Although she has been studying law, she's discovered that she doesn't really have any great interest in the subject. The couple of placements she's done haven't inspired her. She found herself looking at the older people in the office and thinking: 'I don't want to end up like you – working all day, no fun, just motivated by money.' The realisation that she is not passionate about the subject she's been studying for nearly three years is rather depressing. Now what? Jas would like to travel a bit, but what about after? There is no clear picture in her mind about what kind of life she wants: what kind of career, where to live. Instead, there's just a fuzzy picture, made up of bits and pieces of things she might do, but nothing clear or concrete. She's starting to wonder if she might apply to do a Master's for a year while she thinks things through.

AFTER STUDY – NOW WHAT?

Coming to the end of full-time study is a time of major transition in life. For most undergraduates who have gone straight into higher education after school, this is when the pre-established, socially approved signposts begin to disappear from the road. Until now, there hasn't really been much need to think about 'what next'. Instead, the path has been pretty clear: GCSEs, A-levels, university … The biggest decisions are likely to have been what A-levels to take, then which university to apply to and which subject to study. Even for mature students, coming to the end of studies can raise big questions about what direction to take: Stay in an existing job? Wait for a promotion? Perhaps make a bold step and strike off in a completely new direction? Sometimes, as Jas has found, people get to the end of a course with the disturbing realisation that they are no longer interested in the subject and have no desire to make a career in a related field. I've seen medical students, approaching the end of a five-year training, who know that they simply do not want to go into medicine but who feel huge guilt and anxiety about telling family they will not be pursuing what, to others, may seem like a dream career.

A potential risk inherent in pursuing higher education is that it can seem like an end in itself. The relief at getting onto a course at a good university, the pride at being the first in your family to go to university, or the pleasure derived from getting good grades in your work, can disguise the fact that the years you spend at university are stepping-stones to whatever comes next. Of course, learning and studying can be hugely satisfying (or, alternatively, stressful and anxiety-provoking) in themselves, but at some point all courses come to an end. The sense of purpose derived from 'being a student' comes to an end too. The identity you've had as a student disappears, leaving a gap that has, somehow, to be filled.

I have met many postgraduate students (as well as some academics) who simply cannot face the thought of leaving the institutional life of academia. For them, stepping out into the unknown feels too much. As such, they apply, as Jas is contemplating, for Master's courses, then PhDs, and then, sometimes, for jobs as postdoc researchers. Of course, not everyone who does postgraduate study is avoiding engaging with the uncertainty of the outside world, but it's not infrequently a part of a person's motivation for pursuing a further degree without first taking time out to explore the world of work.

FREEDOM AND ANXIETY

The French existential philosopher Jean-Paul Sartre famously stated that human beings are 'condemned to be free' (Sartre, 1946). This may sound strange – surely freedom is a good thing? And yet, as you approach the end of a well-trodden path (your studies) and are forced to make adult decisions about your life, you may well agree with Sartre that freedom can be a burden. Wouldn't it be nice if someone – a counsellor, a careers adviser, your parents, anyone – could tell you what to do that will make you happy and successful? The desire for security and safety is very strong indeed in all of us and the absence of a clearly defined route unnerving. In fact, Sartre argues, most people live in 'bad faith' and reject their freedom, instead preferring to be told what to do, what to think, how to live. This feels safer – less terrifying – but is, ultimately, inauthentic, a second-hand way of living according to other people's norms and rules. We can, if we are not mindful of the competing pressure from within and without, end up living a life that brings little satisfaction or joy.

Being human, as we've seen throughout this book, is not easy. To live well, to be able to respond to life rather than simply reacting according to the primitive instincts of our reptilian brain, is not a simple thing to do. That part of the brain values security and survival above all else. And so, inevitably, as you approach the end of your studies, you will be starting to think about fundamental aspects of security such as having enough money, having somewhere nice to live, finding a partner with whom to share your life. These things can very easily become 'musts': 'I *must* get a good job'; 'I *must* know what I want to do with the rest of my life'; 'I *must* have my future planned out'. We *grasp* security and certainty and *avoid* the anxiety that naturally arises from our new-found, but possibly unwelcome, freedom. Ultimately, perhaps, we want control. We hope that our degrees will earn us security, both financial and emotional, and that our lives will be fulfilling and meaningful. This is all very human, normal and common.

And yet, the search for security and control can inhibit us and steer us away from taking the risks that will enable us to live more authentically. Finding our own path and our own sense of purpose is a challenge we all face – balancing security with risk, conformity with freedom, outward success with inner satisfaction. Furthermore, a sense of wanting to make the *right* choices in life, of finding the *right path*, can also be extremely inhibiting. If there is one right path for me to take, one right job, one right partner, then the stakes are indeed very high. What if I miss the path? What if I don't get the job I've set my heart on? What if someone rejects me when I express a desire to be with them?

MINDFUL EXERCISE

Get a notebook or open a new file on your computer. Give it a heading: 'My fears about the future'.

Over the next week or so, as you engage in formal mindfulness practice (see Chapter 3), notice, without judging yourself, thoughts that arise about the future. Without interrupting your practice, at a later moment write down these thoughts so that you become really aware of them and familiar with any anxieties that are driving those thoughts. You may find that you are thinking or worrying a lot about a career, or a relationship, or accommodation – or something else. Write these thoughts down, using the following format:

Your thought: 'I'll never earn enough money to afford my own place to live.'

You write: '*I'm aware that I have the thought* that I'll never earn enough money to afford my own place to live.'

Your thought: 'Why can't I figure out what I want to do with my life?'

You write: '*I'm aware that I have the thought* that I should know what to do with my life.'

Writing *'I'm aware that I have the thought that ...'* is important, even though it may seem a rather mechanical process. What you are doing here is developing awareness of thoughts as *thoughts*; thoughts as repetitive, often fear-based mental impulses. Behind, above, below and around the thought is your awareness. In other words, you are not just your thoughts. There is an observing, aware part of you that exists apart from the content of your thinking, monkey mind. This is the part of you that you are developing in practising mindfulness. You are slowly learning to become aware, nurturing this non-reactive, holding part of your being. With greater awareness you can recognise when thoughts are taking you too far ahead of yourself, disappearing into unhelpful, fear-based fantasies, and gently learn to let those stories go.

LUCK: THE UNACKNOWLEDGED FACTOR

When I was at university as an undergraduate, I studied modern languages, history and literature – Latin American history and literature to be precise. At the time, I never gave much thought to the future. There seemed to be a belief that simply having a degree was a passport to a bright, successful future. I had vague notions of working in the travel industry, perhaps an airline or a hotel, but nothing very specific. When I graduated, the economic environment was poor and I quickly discovered that, far from finding employers lining up to take advantage of my great gifts in the field of Latin American history, I faced rejection after rejection. I started applying for pretty much anything that seemed remotely possible. Virtually none of the jobs I was going for were 'graduate' jobs – any school-leaver could have done them, and probably better because they did not have the sense of entitlement a degree had unhelpfully bestowed on me. Eventually, after a year of unemployment, I made a decision to retrain as a teacher of English as a foreign language, and spent the next five years teaching abroad. It was fun, and it was good experience to live abroad and use the languages I'd been studying. But by the time I was in my late twenties, I began to realise more strongly that I had no real idea of what my future was going to be. I returned to the UK, took a menial job which I hated and began, very slowly, to realise that what I wanted to do was to work with people. I began to wish I'd done psychology at university, but it felt too late to start another degree at that point. Instead, over the next few years, I did part-time counselling courses – certificates, diplomas – and then trained as a relationship therapist with a large charity for whom I did several years' voluntary work. This was followed by a part-time Master's degree in counselling which led to my first full-time paid position as a therapist when I was thirty-nine. Several years later, I did a doctorate in psychotherapy. I was fifty when I was awarded that. Along the way, I became an accredited psychotherapist, headed a large university counselling service and started a private therapy practice. I took on the editorship of a counselling journal, and started to become involved in assessing the work of trainee counsellors.

Why am I telling you about *my* career journey? Mainly to emphasise that if you are not sure about what you want to do with your life when you leave university, you are not alone. In fact, this is extremely common. Also, that going on to develop a career in a field completely unrelated to your degree subject is not uncommon either. Sometimes our choices are constrained by the economic environment in which we happen to find ourselves when we eventually graduate. My experience is not, I believe, uncommon: try one career possibility, realise it's not what you like and try something else. Discover a course about something you're interested in and keep going. Frequently, a career emerges slowly and the 'path' is often only seen in retrospect. If anyone had told me on my graduation day when I was twenty that I would become a therapist I simply could not have foreseen how this would be possible. Even now, I do not have a sense of having 'followed a path'; I do not have my next five years mapped out. Rather, I have learnt that in life luck seems to have as much to do with our careers and happiness as does skill or planning. 'Luck' is, perhaps, not often acknowledged as a major player in how our lives turn out (and, depending on your faith background, you may frame what

I term 'luck' differently). Yet it seems undeniable that many of the openings in our lives do not emerge because of our careful planning and ability to make the 'right' choices, but as the result of trial and error, learning from our mistakes, and taking advantage of opportunities when they arise. The reality for many people is that their careers and future lives emerge along paths which they would likely never have contemplated at the point of leaving full-time education.

Having a five-year plan is not a bad thing. Cultivating thoughts and dreams about the kind of career you think you would like to build can be very helpful and many graduates *will* find work in an area related to their studies. Making plans, consulting careers advisors, talking to mentors and others who have worked in professions we are considering, all of this makes good sense. Mindfulness encourages us to hold our plans and hopes more lightly, on an open palm rather than in a clenched fist. It asks us to acknowledge that much of life is beyond our control, that nothing is permanent and that change is happening every moment, every breath. And to face the reality that our lives are short, and that what counts more than financial or hierarchical success is developing clarity about our values and being true to those.

MINDFUL EXERCISE

If the prospect of creating an achievement-based plan for your life feels daunting, perhaps you are putting the cart before the horse. Goals such as 'To be earning £100k by the time I'm twenty-five' or 'To retire at fifty-five' may or may not be possible; much will depend on circumstances beyond your control as well as aspects of life you cannot yet foresee.

● ● ● ●

Spend some time creating a different kind of plan, based on developing greater alignment between your values and the work you hope to do and the kind of relationships you would like to develop. Instead of goals that can be checked off a list once achieved, identify priorities that will serve as your compass as you navigate your way through life – priorities that you do have some control over. For example, your priorities might include:

- to continue to develop self-compassion for yourself and others;

- to develop a mindfulness practice that nourishes a deeper appreciation of your life as it is right now;

- to clarify the values that will guide you to become the person you aspire to be;

- to express love and practical care for your family and the people you encounter throughout your working life.

Your priorities are yours; there is no right or wrong. Provided they do not involve exploiting others or the planet, you are free to move in whatever direction is 'right' for you at this point. Your priorities will change as you go through life. For example, if you become a parent, you might find yourself wanting to provide as much security for your children as possible and as a result being willing to take on work that otherwise would seem boring or exhausting. Without priorities (your sense of what really matters in life), a high-powered career can feel pointless; money alone is unlikely to provide lasting satisfaction or meaning for your life. Priorities – values – change the complexion of external circumstances, giving meaning in otherwise difficult situations.

Use your list of priorities to regularly assess whether a particular job opportunity, relationship or other opportunity is likely to help you fulfil your hopes for the kind of person you want to be.

THE URGENCY FOR MINDFUL AWARENESS

One of the concerns I hear from students when they are beginning to understand more of what mindfulness is – and isn't – focuses on whether developing awareness and learning to see thoughts as 'just' thoughts will undermine their ability to study, make plans, deal with challenges. It seems that they imagine that taking time to 'just be' might sap them of intellectual vigour – a quality that is prized perhaps above all at university. It's a reasonable issue to raise; after all, no one would want to surrender their amazing human ability to solve problems, think creatively and plan ahead for what needs to be done. 'Maybe', their thinking seems to run, 'if I spend too much time being mindful I'll end up being no practical use.'

Yet, in fact, what mindfulness has the potential to help us with is distinguishing between thoughts that are helpful for us and those that are distinctly unhelpful or pointless. This is particularly true when we are talking about the future. We tend to have very vivid imaginations whereby we can conjure up scenarios which are either wildly over-optimistic or depressingly gloomy. We might enjoy a fantasy where our first boss quickly decides that we are *the* outstanding new recruit who deserves quick promotion and the company car of our choice; and we might feel deeply upset if we get lost in thoughts that have us forever stuck in menial jobs with no secure income or prospects for security. Mindfulness enables us to *wake up* from such thoughts and to recognise them for what they are: *just* thoughts.

There is a Zen story that illustrates how, without awareness, our minds can lead us along pathways we have never fully understood or considered:

'A man is riding a horse that is galloping frantically, as if he has to be somewhere important, as soon as possible. A bystander sees this and asks the man, "*Where are you going?*"

"I don't know," the rider replies, "*ask the horse!*"' (Openskyzen.blogspot)

Here, our minds are depicted as out-of-control horses, leading us somewhere we may not wish to go. Our thinking minds, invaluable and amazing as they are, can also lead us into trouble.

Where do thoughts come from? What is the difference between a thought and a dream? Can we control our thoughts? Should we take all our thoughts seriously? These are questions we have discussed in mindfulness groups that I have run for students. It has been estimated that the average person will have between sixty and eighty *thousand* thoughts a day (Barok, 2016). I'm not sure how anyone actually makes a calculation like this, but whatever the reality, it's true that we are all thinking all the time. It's what our brains/minds do. And our thoughts are associative. In other words, one thought leads to another by association: 'I like that blue jacket. Blue is my favourite colour. I wonder what colour hair I'll have when I'm fifty? Ugh. who wants to be fifty? I think Dad is fifty-two. Oh, I should call Dad …' and so on. It seems that we have little control over the thoughts our minds produce for us. Yet, we can learn not to get lost in thoughts that are unhelpful for us. *If thoughts are like birds, your mind is a tree. You can't stop the birds from landing on the branches, but you don't have to feed them.*

In this sense, mindfulness helps us to distinguish between thoughts to cultivate and thoughts to let just 'be'. It can help us to see when we are basing future scenarios on a false sense of ability to control what is beyond our influence, or when particular worries serve no purpose because there is nothing we can actually do to assuage them. We can also become familiar with repetitive, unhelpful patterns of thought that, if nurtured, will only land us in trouble.

There may be a sense in which mindfulness is seen in Western culture as a 'nice' thing to do, a kind of relaxing hobby that we fit in as and when we can around our busy schedules. However, the way I see it is very different. Because our thinking minds – those powerful, often primitive organisms – control so many of our emotions and behaviours, there might even be a sense of urgency in devoting time to developing awareness of thoughts and feelings. Without this awareness, we can be riders on a horse we have no control over: our unruly minds create all sorts of thoughts and imagined future scenarios for us. Thoughts become actions; actions become habits; habits become character. Developing an awareness of thoughts as thoughts, and an ability to discern which thoughts are helpful and which unhelpful is not something you do for fun: it is more serious than that. Some Buddhist texts speak of meditating 'like your hair is on fire' (Chödrön, 2010): one of our tendencies as human beings is to think we have lots of time to eventually get round to doing what is important. This saying is meant to wake us up to the reality that we never know how much time we have in this life and that each moment is precious. Mindfulness is not a hobby; it is not meant to be something we pick up and put down according to how we feel. It is something to bring our best energies to – not straining to achieve some imagined, enlightened state, but practising with seriousness and dedication. Perhaps this might become one of your priorities as you look ahead.

MINDFULNESS AND AUTHENTIC LIVING

When Jasminder had spent some time in formal mindfulness, she began to realise that she was stuck in thoughts about how the future 'should' be. There were thoughts and beliefs that she should become a solicitor and earn a lot of money, drive a fancy car and generally be considered a success by friends and family. The trouble was, this kind of life did not bring her any feelings of joy or excitement, yet she could not see any way of breaking out of these expectations. She allowed herself to start to explore her own priorities – the values that she wanted her life to embody and express. She realised that what she found so unappealing about law was how people seemed to use it in ways that, to her, appeared dishonest or unhelpfully combative: she could see how primitive brain thinking – territorialism, attacking others, defending a position that seemed unreasonable – could predominate in the profession. Although it was very scary, Jas started to explore other possible careers that were more in keeping with her values: a previously unacknow-ledged interest in midwifery began to emerge more strongly. Despite the fear, this felt 'authentic' and life-affirming to Jas and she actually began to feel a difference within her body, a kind of tingling warmth, as she allowed herself to acknowledge that her future might be quite different from the one she had been trying to squeeze herself into.

Mindfulness, I believe, is a vital skill. Although it emerges from a Buddhist context, other philosophical traditions and religions emphasise the importance of strengthening our awareness of contemplation. Islam, Christianity, Judaism and other faiths all have mystic traditions that point in similar ways to the importance of stepping out of the flow of thoughts produced by our minds and being still, or

to put it boldly, contemplation [mindfulness] is the only ultimate answer to the unreal and insane world that our financial systems and our advertising culture and our chaotic and unexamined emotions encourage us to inhabit. To learn contemplative prayer [mindfulness] is to learn what we need so as to live truthfully and honestly and lovingly. It is a deeply revolutionary matter. (Williams, 2012)

As you contemplate your future beyond your time as a student, I hope that however you incorporate mindfulness into your life, you will find it to be a life-long source of inner support and wisdom, richly rewarding the time and effort you commit to practising. As with anything worth pursuing such as exercise, diet and career, persistence and determination are required. Mindfulness is not a competition; straining is not helpful, whether by forcing yourself to sit for long periods in the hope that 'more time = more results', or by judging the outcomes of your practice by whether they 'felt good'. It is an ongoing opportunity to wake up to reality – pleasant, unpleasant and neutral – and to become your own best ally: increasingly free from unhelpful thinking patterns, rooted in self-compassion and committed to act in accordance with your values towards the people who accompany you on your journey through life.

May you be well.

May you be healthy and strong.

May you be free from mental and physical suffering.

May you be safe and protected.

May you know deep compassion.

May you be happy.

QUESTIONS FOR REFLECTION

1. What is the best future for yourself that you can imagine? Allow yourself to envision a house, a career, a relationship that you think would bring most meaning and satisfaction to you, and contribute to the wellbeing of others. As you do, be aware of any internal voice that tells you: 'You'll never be able to do that', 'That'll never happen'. How might you stop yourself from living as authentically as possible?

2. What values seem most important to you in life? Take some time to reflect on what, for you, gives life meaning. As you contemplate your future, let your values guide you to live in the most meaningful way possible.

3. What anxieties does your mind create for you when you think about your future? Worries about a career? Housing? Relationships? Do these anxieties help you to take meaningful action of some kind? If not, gently encourage yourself to see your mind's stories as emerging from your primitive, reptilian brain: not the truth.

FURTHER READING

Tara Brach (2013) *True Refuge: Finding Peace and Freedom in Your Own Awakened Heart.* Carlsbad, CA Hay House.

In this book, the author encourages us to develop confidence in our own wisdom and ability to respond wisely and compassionately to whatever life brings our way.

Jack Kornfield (2002) *A Path with Heart.* London: Rider.

A leading American Buddhist teacher of mindfulness, Jack Kornfield here guides the reader through many of the challenges that await each of us as we continue our journey through life.

REFERENCES

Barok, S. (2016) Did you know ... you have between 50,000 and 70,000 thoughts per day ... Available at: https://www.huffingtonpost.co.uk/shahilla-barok/did-you-knowyou-have-betw_b_11819532.html (accessed 27 December 2018).

Chödrön, P. (2010) 10 Steps to Finding Your Happy Place (and Staying There). Available at: http://10stepsoffindingyourhappyplace.blogspot.com/2010/02/your-hair-is-on-fire.html (paragraph 2) (accessed 27 January 2019).

Machado, A. (1912) *Proverbios y cantares XXIX* [Proverbs and Songs 29], *Campos de Castilla;* trans. Craige, B. J. in *Selected Poems of Antonio Machado* (1979) Baton Rouge, LA: Louisiana State University Press.

Sartre, J.P. (1946) Man is condemned to be free. Available at: https://wmpeople.wm.edu/asset/index/cvance/sartre (accessed 2 January 2019).

Taming my wild horse mind. Available at: http://openskyzen.blogspot.com/2011/06/taming-my-wild-horse-mind.html (accessed 1 April 2019).

Williams, R. (2012) The Archbishop of Canterbury's address to the thirteenth ordinary general assembly of the Synod of Bishops on the New Evangelisation for the Transmission of the Christian Faith, 10 October. Available at: http://rowanwilliams.archbishopofcanterbury.org/articles.php/2645/archbishops-address-to-the-synod-of-bishops-in-rome (accessed 30 December 2018).

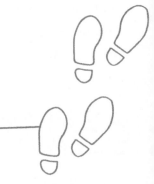

AFTERWORD
TAKING MINDFULNESS FURTHER

I hope that after reading this book and practising some of the mindfulness exercises, you are beginning to get a sense of how mindfulness can enhance your life. As I made clear at the start, for me mindfulness is not a 'self-improvement' technique, something designed to make you more productive, more efficient, more successful. Instead, it is a way of being that allows you to get out of your own way, to rise above the incessant chattering of your anxious mind and to inhabit all of your physical senses more fully. It is an anchor to reality, whether that is pleasant, unpleasant or simply neutral. Mindfulness ultimately offers a way out of the suffering that we so often load onto the inescapable pain of existence.

Getting out of our own way is not a once-and-for-all occurrence. And yet the self-imposed limitations created by our upbringing, our culture, our life-experience can prevent us from encountering life in all its wonder, sadness and joy. We are addicted to thinking and imagine that our rational mind can solve every emotional problem we encounter. Often, thinking about our problems is like pouring petrol onto a fire to put it out: we simply make things worse. In mindfulness, we deliberately step out of the thought stream and come fully into our bodies and senses – allowing ourselves to encounter reality-as-it-is.

'Simple – not easy' is a phrase you'll have seen repeated throughout this book and is one I want to echo here. The *theory* of mindfulness is very simple; the *putting it into practice* takes determination and commitment – and this is where support can be so helpful. If you would like to strengthen your experience of mindfulness and of what it can offer, there are different ways to do this, which are briefly outlined here:

Join a mindfulness group. This is, in my view, essential to maintain your motivation and commitment. Being with others who are equally determined and equally struggling can help you to integrate mindfulness into your life. Have a look on campus noticeboards – the chaplaincy might be a good place to start, or a Buddhist society if there is one – for groups that are meeting where you study. Some counselling services also run mindfulness groups that offer an excellent way to learn more about this path in the company of like-minded people.

Explore apps. There are many excellent apps that can support you in practising formal mindfulness, for example Headspace and Buddhify. Some make a monthly charge – others a one-off fee. You may find the guided meditations that these apps offer a useful input for you; they enable you to meditate or engage in other forms of mindfulness on the train or bus and while waiting for lectures. I would encourage you not to rely totally on apps – the interpersonal support of a real-time group is very hard to beat – but they are certainly a worthwhile area to explore.

Go on retreat. In this book, you have encountered short mindfulness exercises designed to be brief enough to work around a busy schedule. It can be a wonderful experience to dedicate a whole weekend or week to stepping away from that schedule and allow yourself to experience longer stretches of time to allow your mind to settle and for deeper clarity to emerge. There are many mindfulness retreats on offer: I suggest you start with a short one (perhaps just a day) and then, depending on how you find that, try longer periods. Always trust your experience on retreat: if you ever feel uncomfortable about the style of leadership, do allow yourself to try somewhere else until you sense that the 'fit' is good for you.

Do a MBSR or MBCT eight-week course. If you search online for mindfulness-based stress reduction (MBSR) or mindfulness-based cognitive therapy (MBCT) courses you will find details of teacher-led courses that will give you input into managing stress and/or depression from a mindfulness perspective. Entirely secular in approach, these courses offer a good framework to build mindfulness skills into your daily life.

Read. Reading about mindfulness can be very helpful – provided reading doesn't become a substitute for practising. There are many suggestions for further reading at the end of each chapter in this book, and selecting one of these books to study would be an excellent commitment to building your understanding and appreciation of what mindfulness has to offer.

I hope that you continue to explore and experience mindfulness for yourself; it is an approach to life that can deepen your appreciation of your time on this planet while enabling you to reduce the pull of automatic, reactionary thinking and to avoid self-imposed suffering. I wish you well.

All the vignettes included in this book are typical of issues facing students; all are fictitious.

INDEX